# TABLE OF CONTENTS

© Disney

# Walt Disney Archives

500 So. Buena Vista St. | Burbank, California 91521-1200

FOREWORD

Dear Researcher:

Thank you so much for your interest in The Walt Disney Company.

As you might imagine, we frequently receive requests from people who are interested in studying the background and history of our many famous and beloved animated characters. Disney's cartoon casts have not only delighted and entertained millions around the world and across the generations; they have become the backbone of our entertainment endeavors.

Whether it is performing a sprightly musical number in an animated short subject, starring in a feature film, posing for a poster or product label, acting in a comic book story, or greeting millions of visitors in Disney parks worldwide, our ensemble of animated actors have shown remarkable longevity and versatility in their work over a long period of time.

Pursuant to your request, the Walt Disney Archives is not generally open to the public for research, but fortunately the Walt Disney Feature Animation Casting Department, a division of the Walt Disney Studios, recently made me aware of the enclosed files, which I am delighted to provide for you.

These remarkable dossiers have been accumulated, updated, annotated, and maintained within the Casting Offices over many years for reference and for the use of producers, directors, story people, and writers who are developing new projects and who wish to consider casting one of our established company of performers. I think you'll find them perfect as a primer on a singular cast of characters and an entertaining and informative collection of data, background, statistics, and trivia.

Best of luck!

Dave Smith
Founding Director
Walt Disney Archives

# MICKEY MOUSE

*The first Mickey Mouse comic strips were drawn by Ub Iwerks and published in 1930.*

## THE FACTS

**NAME:** Mickey Mouse

**BIRTHDAY:** November 18, 1928

**SHORTS:** Red

**SHOES:** Yellow

**VOICED BY:**
Walt Disney (1928–1947);
Jimmy Macdonald (1947–1983);
Wayne Allwine (1983–present)

**SIGNIFICANT OTHER:**
Minnie Mouse

**CLOSE RELATIVES:** Morty and Ferdie (nephews)

**DOG:** Pluto Pup

**DESCRIPTION:** Friendly, funny, charming, and talented

**WORKS WELL WITH:** Minnie Mouse, Donald Duck, Goofy, Pluto Pup

**FAVORITE PHRASES:** "Oh boy!" "That sure is swell!" "Gosh!" "Aw, gee" "See ya soon!"

*The first merchandise to feature Mickey Mouse was a child's school tablet in 1929.*

*The Encyclopedia Britannica gave Mickey Mouse his own entry in 1934.*

## FROM THE DESK OF

### WALT DISNEY

Mickey was simply a little personality assigned to the purposes of laughter.

← *Mickey Mouse Ingersoll pocket watch.*

**MICKEY MOUSE DEBUTED IN THE CHARMING 1928 ANIMATED SHORT** "Steamboat Willie" and went on to become the familiar symbol of the Walt Disney Studios. A cheerful rodent, soon clad in familiar white gloves and red shorts, Mickey starred in dozens of cartoon shorts and became a superstar during the Great Depression.

Mickey was the first cartoon star to express a unique personality and to be constantly kept in character. Walt thought of him from the start as a distinct individual, not just a symbol performing a comedy routine. Mickey became one of the great actors of his time, playing everything from a fireman to a giant-killer, a cowboy to an inventor, a detective to a plumber. Technically and artistically, Mickey Mouse cartoons were far superior to other contemporary cartoons, and gave life to an extended family of animated stars.

Mickey's popularity spawned a Mickey Mouse Club in 1929, which met every Saturday for an afternoon of cartoons and games in local theaters. The several million Mouse Clubbers had a secret handshake, a special greeting, a code of behavior, and even a club song, "Minnie's Yoo-Hoo."

## CAREER

**FIRST FILM:**
"Plane Crazy," 1928

**PUBLIC DEBUT:**
"Steamboat Willie," 1928

**FILMOGRAPHY (HIGHLIGHTS):**
"The Chain Gang," 1930
  (first appearance of Pluto Pup)
"Mickey's Orphans," 1931
  (Oscar nominee)
"The Band Concert," 1935
  (first Mickey cartoon
  in Technicolor)
"Country Cousin," 1936
  (Oscar winner)
"Brave Little Tailor," 1938
  (Oscar nominee)
*Fantasia*, 1940
  (Mickey's first feature film)
"The Simple Things," 1953
  (Mickey's last short cartoon
  for the following 42 years)
*The Mickey Mouse Club*, 1955
  (Mickey's series TV debut)
*Who Framed Roger Rabbit*, 1988
  (cameo)
*The Prince and the Pauper*, 1990
*Runaway Brain*, 1995
  (Oscar nominee)
*Mickey Mouse Works*, 1999
  (TV series)
*Mickey's Once Upon*
  *A Christmas*, 1999
*Fantasia/2000*
*Disney's House of Mouse*, 2001
  (TV series)
*Mickey's House of Villains*, 2002
*Mickey's Twice Upon*
  *A Christmas*, 2004
*The Three Musketeers*, 2004

**HONORS AND AWARDS:**
A special Academy Award was
given to Walt Disney for
the creation of Mickey Mouse
in 1932.

The League of Nations presented
Walt Disney with a special
medal in 1935 to recognize that
Mickey was "a symbol of
universal goodwill."

On November 18, 1978, in honor
of his 50th birthday, he became
the first cartoon character to
have a star on the Hollywood
Walk of Fame.

---

With his cheery attitude and unflagging optimism, Mickey has always held the spotlight, remaining one of the world's best-known and best-loved cartoon performers. He became an international personality whose success laid the foundation upon which Walt Disney built his creative organization.

After 1950, Mickey appeared only rarely in films and instead settled into his role as Disney's goodwill ambassador to the world. Today, he welcomes millions of visitors annually at the Disneyland Resort, Walt Disney World Resort, Tokyo Disneyland Resort, Disneyland Resort Paris, and Hong Kong Disneyland. Mickey has greeted kings and presidents, prime ministers and princes, athletes, film and TV stars, and millions of just plain folks.

One of the finest tributes to Mickey was given by Walt Disney himself when, on his first *Disneyland* TV show, Walt said, "I hope we never lose sight of one fact...that this was all started by a mouse."

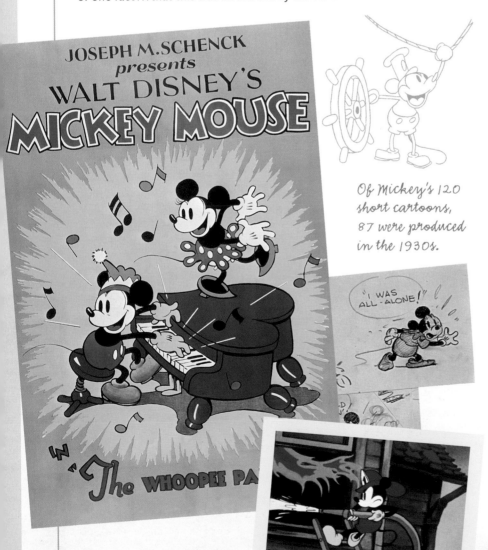

JOSEPH M. SCHENCK
presents
WALT DISNEY'S
MICKEY MOUSE

*Of Mickey's 120 short cartoons, 87 were produced in the 1930s.*

"I WAS ALL-ALONE!"

# MINNIE MOUSE

*The first voice of Minnie Mouse after Walt was Marcellite Garner, from the Ink and Paint Department at the Disney Studio.*

## THE FACTS

**NAME:** Minerva Mouse

**VOICED BY:**
Walt Disney (early shorts);
Marcellite Garner (1928–1940);
Thelma Boardman (1940–1942);
Ruth Clifford (1942–1952);
Russi Taylor (1986–present)

**SIGNIFICANT OTHER:**
Mickey Mouse

**FATHER:** Marcus Mouse

**GRANDFATHER:** Marshall Mouse

**GRANDMOTHER:** Matilda Mouse

**CLOSE RELATIVES:** Millie
and Melody (nieces)

**CAT:** Figaro

**DESCRIPTION:** Pretty, peppy,
and playful

**WORKS WELL WITH:** Mickey
Mouse, Figaro, Pluto Pup

**FAVORITE PHRASES:** "Why,
hello!" "Aren't you sweet!"
"Yoo-hoo!" "Oh, Mickey..."

*Timeless fashion choices: bloomers, polka dots, pumps.*

SMACK
SMACK

**STARRING ALONGSIDE MICKEY FROM HIS VERY FIRST FILM WAS HIS TRUE** lady love, Minnie Mouse.

Although they have never married, their nearly eight-decade romance is certainly one of the longest in Hollywood history. Mickey and Minnie both debuted in "Steamboat Willie" (1928), and over the years Minnie has been featured in seventy-three cartoons.

Oddly, although she took a featured role in so many cartoon shorts, Minnie was never given her own cartoon "star label." Mickey Mouse (of course), Donald Duck, Goofy—even Pluto—got their own "sunburst" starring title cards in the shorts produced regularly from 1932 until 1965, but not poor Minnie!

In 1986, Minnie was finally given her due, updated with 1980s fashion (and independent attitude), and called "Totally Minnie." She was featured in new Minnie merchandise, a "Totally Minnie Parade" at Disneyland, a CD of pop and rock songs, a *Totally Minnie* TV special—and even a music video co-starring Elton John.

*Minnie's comic strip debut was in the very first story in the* <u>Mickey Mouse</u> *daily strip, "Lost on a Desert Island" (1930).*

**FILM DEBUT:**
"Steamboat Willie," 1928

**FILMOGRAPHY (HIGHLIGHTS):**
"The Gallopin' Gaucho," 1928
"Plane Crazy," 1928
"The Barn Dance," 1928
"The Plow Boy," 1929
"Mickey's Follies," 1929
"Pioneer Days," 1930
"Blue Rhythm," 1931
"The Beach Party," 1931
"Mickey's Orphans," 1931
"Mickey's Revue," 1932
"The Whoopee Party," 1932
"The Pet Store," 1933
"Two-Gun Mickey," 1934
"Hawaiian Holiday," 1937
"Brave Little Tailor," 1938
   (Oscar nominee)
"Figaro and Frankie," 1947
"Crazy over Daisy," 1950
"Pluto's Christmas Tree," 1952
*Mickey's Christmas Carol*, 1983
*Who Framed Roger Rabbit*, 1988
   (cameo)
*Runaway Brain*, 1995
*Mickey Mouse Works*, 1999
   (TV series)
*Mickey's Once Upon
   A Christmas*, 1999
*Disney's House of Mouse*, 2001
   (TV series)
*Mickey's House of Villains*, 2002
*Mickey's Twice Upon
   A Christmas*, 2004

*In "The Picnic" (November 14, 1930), Minnie introduces her boyfriend to her new pet dog, "Rover." This is actually Pluto making his first appearance as an individual character.*

*The comic strip story "The Gleam" (published January 19–May 2, 1942) by Merrill De Maris and Floyd Gottfredson first gave her full name as Minerva Mouse.*

# GOOFY

*Beginning in 1953, Goofy starred in his own limited series of comic book adventures.*

*"gawrsh!"*

## THE FACTS

**NAME:** Goofy Goof

**ALSO KNOWN AS:** George Geef, Dippy Dawg, Dippy the Goof

**VOICED BY:** Pinto Colvig (1932–1938; 1944–1965); George Johnson (1939–1943); Bob Jackman (1951); Hal Smith (1983); Tony Pope (1988); Will Ryan (1988); Bill Farmer (1986–present)

**SIGNIFICANT OTHER:** Occasionally seen with Clarabelle Cow

Mr. Geef had a wife and son

**CLOSE RELATIVE:** Max (son)

**DESCRIPTION:** Gangly, curious, and laid-back; a philosopher of the barbershop variety

**WORKS WELL WITH:** Mickey Mouse, Donald Duck

FOR MORE THAN SEVENTY YEARS, GOOFY—THE AWKWARD, TOOTHY, GOOD-spirited Everyman of the Disney characters—has been a top performer, beginning with a bit part in a Disney short, and eventually becoming a major media star in print, television, theme parks, and a variety of merchandise.

Walt Disney often described the type of physical humor used in the Walt Disney Studio's cartoons as being "goofy," and with "Orphan's Benefit" (1934), that name officially stuck to this affable character. Goofy's personality really began to take shape in the 1935 cartoon "Moving Day," in which animator Art Babbitt built up Goofy's role and gave his character definition. And thus, a new Disney star was born—loose-jointed, vapory of brain, and easily distracted, but happy to help anyone (even when this merely creates confusion) and generally accepting of whatever happens as being for the best.

In 1995, Goofy became a motion picture star in his own film, *A Goofy Movie*, which featured the lovable goof trying to bond with his teenage son, Max.

*Goofy's positive, "I'll try anything" attitude was the focus of the 1980s Sport Goofy athletic programs.*

Goofy became the first of the classic "Fab Five" (Mickey, Minnie, Donald, Pluto, and Goofy) to star in a television series of his own, with the premiere of Buena Vista Television's Goof Troop in September 1992.

↓ with Max

WALT DISNEY'S
GOOFY and WILBUR
A "MICKEY MOUSE"

HOW TO FISH

Comic strips first called the character Dippy Dawg, and in 1938 Dippy the Goof, but eventually his name changed to Goofy.

PLANES NEED GASOLINE

SHARE YOUR CAR
FOR YOUR COUNTRY

© WALT DISNEY

## CAREER

**FILM DEBUT:**
"Mickey's Revue," 1932

**FILMOGRAPHY (HIGHLIGHTS):**
"Goofy and Wilbur," 1939
"Goofy's Glider," 1940
"The Art of Self Defense," 1941
"How to Play Baseball," 1942
"How to Play Football," 1944
   (Oscar nominee)
"Tiger Trouble," 1945
"African Diary," 1945
"Californy 'er Bust," 1945
"Hockey Homicide," 1945
"The Big Wash," 1948
"Goofy Gymnastics," 1949
"Motor Mania," 1950
"Get Rich Quick," 1951
"Fathers Are People," 1951
"No Smoking," 1951
"Two-Gun Goofy," 1952
"Teachers Are People," 1952
"Aquamania," 1961
   (Oscar nominee)
*Mickey Mouse Works,* 1999
   (TV series)
*Mickey's Once Upon
   A Christmas,* 1999
*Disney's House of Mouse,* 2001
   (TV series)
*Mickey's House of Villains,* 2002
*Mickey's Twice Upon
   A Christmas,* 2004
*The Three Musketeers,* 2004

**HONORS AND AWARDS:**
Sport Goofy was named the official mascot of the French Olympic team.

Sport Goofy was endorsed by the German Sport Association.

# DONALD DUCK

## THE FACTS

**NAME:** Donald Fauntleroy Duck

**VOICED BY:** Clarence "Ducky" Nash (1934–1984); Tony Anselmo (1984–present)

**SIGNIFICANT OTHER:** Daisy Duck

**FATHER:** Quackmore Duck

**MOTHER:** Hortense McDuck

**SIBLINGS:** Della Duck (twin sister)

**CLOSE RELATIVES:** Huey, Dewey, and Louie Duck (nephews), Scrooge McDuck (uncle), Gus Goose (cousin)

**LIKES:** Dishing it out

**DISLIKES:** Taking it

**DESCRIPTION:** Hot tempered (listen for trademark **"WAK!"** sound and facial reddening)

**FAVORITE PHRASES:** "Oh, boy! Oh, boy! Oh, boy!" "Hi, toots!" "Aw, phooey!"

**WORKS WELL WITH:** Mickey Mouse, Goofy, Pluto Pup

**DONALD IS PERHAPS THE MOST VERSATILE OF ALL DISNEY CHARACTERS.** Since his debut in 1934's "The Wise Little Hen," he's proven that he can carry off a variety of roles. Exceptions are dumb roles and gentlemen parts—he is too smart and active to play the former, and as for the latter, he just can't be bothered. He is vain, cocky, and boastful, and loves to heckle others, but if the tables are turned, he flies into a rage.

Donald's most likeable trait is his determination. In most of his motion pictures, he has some goal to achieve, which he goes after with a vengeance. When attacking a problem, he may be cocky, cautious, or cunning—or all three by turns. Some of his best work is done when he attempts to be cunning. On these occasions, he frequently enjoys temporary success (which goes to his head), but his craftiness always backfires sooner or later.

His well-known quick temper arises in most instances from the frustration of his desires, but ridicule, petty annoyances, impatience, or ruthless destruction of some valued possession

can make him turn the air blue. Even in his wildest rages, though, Donald can be mollified by a little gratification. He is also easily amused, and laughs heartily when he thinks he has caused some person or thing discomfort.

A classic example of Donald's devious side can be found in the 1935 cartoon "The Band Concert," in which he repeatedly disrupts the Mickey Mouse Orchestra's performance of the *William Tell Overture* by playing "Turkey in the Straw"—a moment hailed by critics and loved by Donald fans. He has also made his mark in everything from wartime propaganda movies (including 1943 Oscar winner "Der Fuehrer's Face") to live-action films (with a trademark temper flare in 1988's *Who Framed Roger Rabbit*) to TV series (*DuckTales*, *Quack Pack*) with his recognizable trio of nephews.

Donald should be given dialog sparingly; few people understand his words, and his voice is funny in sound more than content. Still, he is very popular, particularly with adult audiences; his mood swings and humanlike emotions make him easy to identify with. His versatility has afforded him a prolific film and comic book career.

**FROM THE DESK OF**

*WALT DISNEY*

His towering rages, his impotence in the face of obstacles, his protests in the face of injustice, as he sees it—even though he brings disaster on himself—have kept him an audience favorite.

**OFFICIAL** DOCUMENTS

DOWN BY THE POND LIVES DONALD DUCK NO LABOR EVER BOTHERS HIM BECAUSE HE NEVER BOTHERS IT HE'D RATHER, FAR TO DANCE OR SWIM!

## CAREER

**FILM DEBUT:**
"The Wise Little Hen," 1934

**FILMOGRAPHY (HIGHLIGHTS):**
"Good Scouts," 1938
    (Oscar nominee)
"Truant Officer Donald," 1941
    (Oscar nominee)
*Saludos Amigos*, 1943
    (Donald's feature debut)
"Der Fuehrer's Face," 1943
    (Oscar winner)
"Donald's Crime," 1945
    (Oscar nominee)
"Tea for Two Hundred," 1948
    (Oscar nominee)
"Toy Tinkers," 1949
    (Oscar nominee)
"Rugged Bear," 1953
    (Oscar nominee)
"No Hunting," 1955
    (Oscar nominee)
"Donald in Mathmagic Land," 1959
    (Oscar nominee)
"Steel and America," 1965
    (commercial)
*Mickey's Christmas Carol*, 1983
    (Oscar nominee)
*DuckTales*, 1987
    (TV series)
*Who Framed Roger Rabbit*, 1988
    (cameo)
*DuckTales the Movie: Treasure of the Lost Lamp*, 1990
*The Prince and the Pauper*, 1990
*Quack Pack*, 1996
    (TV series)
*Mickey Mouse Works*, 1999
    (TV series)
*Mickey's Once Upon A Christmas*, 1999
*Fantasia/2000*
*Disney's House of Mouse*, 2001
    (TV series)
*Mickey's House of Villains*, 2002
*Mickey's Twice Upon A Christmas*, 2004
*The Three Musketeers*, 2004

**HONORS AND AWARDS:**
Donald was honored on August 10, 2004, with the 2,257th star on the Hollywood Walk of Fame.

Donald Duck

# DAISY DUCK

## THE FACTS

**NAME:** Daisy Duck

**ALSO CREDITED AS:** Donna Duck

**VOICED BY:**
Clarence Nash (early Daisy);
Ruth Peterson;
Gloria Blondell;
Patricia Parris (*Mickey's Christmas Carol*, 1983);
Kath Soucie (*Quack Pack*, 1996);
Tress MacNeille (1999–present)

**SIGNIFICANT OTHER:** Donald Duck (although she has been known to flirt with Gladstone Gander, usually to make Donald jealous)

**RELATIVES:** April, May, and June (nieces); Aunt Matilda, Aunt Drusilla (unseen); Daisy is the sister of Donald's brother-in-law: Daisy's brother had married Donald's twin sister, Della Thelma Duck, and together, the two became the parents of Huey, Dewey, and Louie Duck

**DESCRIPTION:** Mistress of high drama; able to go from coy to flaming just as fast as her beau

**FAVORITE PHRASES:** "Well, I never!" "Oh, Donald..."

**SPECIAL SKILLS:** Sassy sashay; great dresser

**DAISY MADE HER DEBUT IN "DON DONALD" (1937), AND WENT ON TO MAKE** fourteen further film appearances. In the 1996 television series *Quack Pack*, Daisy was presented as an assertive and liberated woman, employed as a television station reporter with Donald as her cameraman.

Daisy shares Donald's temper but has far greater control of it and tends to be more sophisticated than her boyfriend. A woman who knows her mind, she expects to be treated right: candy, flowers, and a night on the town. If Donald won't toe the line, she's not afraid to offer an ultimatum: "Until you develop a more pleasant personality, I don't want to see you again."

Threats notwithstanding, she's confident that Donald will always be back, faults and all. In fact, given the choice between keeping him for herself just as he is or sharing him with the rest of the world, she makes her feelings for Donald very clear.

*Daisy's first appearance in comics was in the Donald Duck daily strip from November 4, 1940.*

*The British magazine Mickey Mouse Weekly featured "Donna Duck" in their comic from May to August 1937.*

The name for _Daisy Duck_ in some other languages:

Danish: _Andersine And_
Finnish: _Iines Ankka_
Italian: _Paperina_
Norwegian: _Dolly Duck_
Portuguese: _Margarida_
Swedish: _Kajsa Anka_

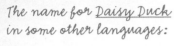

## CAREER

**FILM DEBUT:**
"Don Donald," 1937
  (as "Donna Duck")

**FILMOGRAPHY (HIGHLIGHTS):**
"Mr. Duck Steps Out," 1940
"A Good Time for a Dime," 1941
"The Nifty Nineties," 1941
"Donald's Crime," 1945
"Cured Duck," 1945
"Donald's Double Trouble," 1946
"Dumb Bell of the Yukon," 1946
"Sleepy Time Donald," 1947
"Donald's Dilemma," 1947
"Donald's Dream Voice," 1948
"Crazy Over Daisy," 1950
"Donald's Diary," 1954
_Mickey's Christmas Carol_, 1983
  (Oscar nominee)
_Mickey Mouse Works_, 1999
  (TV series)
_Mickey's Once Upon
  A Christmas_, 1999
_Fantasia/2000_
_Disney's House of Mouse_, 2001
  (TV series)
_Mickey's House of Villains_, 2002
_Mickey's Twice Upon
  A Christmas_, 2004

# PLUTO PUP

Pluto was possibly named after the planet Pluto, which was discovered in 1930, the same year that the character debuted.

## THE FACTS

**NAME:** Pluto Pup

**VOICED BY:**
Pinto Colvig;
Lee Millar, Sr.;
Clarence Nash;
Jim Macdonald;
Bill Farmer

**SIGNIFICANT OTHERS:** Fifi the Peke, Dinah the Dachshund

**SIBLINGS:** In the 1946 animated short "Pluto's Kid Brother," Pluto has a younger brother named K.B.

**CLOSE RELATIVES:** In the 1942 animated short "Pluto Junior," Pluto has a son who is referred to as "Pluto Junior"

**DESCRIPTION:** Loyal, curious, guileless

**DOES NOT WORK WELL WITH:** Flypaper, Butch the Bulldog, Figaro the Kitten, Chip or Dale, Buzz the Bee

**FAVORITE PHRASES:** "Grrr..." "Snort!" "Sniff, sniff, sniff..." "Bark! Bark!"

Pluto had his own Sunday newspaper comic strip during the late 1930s.

STUDIO CIRCULATION ONLY

**MICKEY'S FAITHFUL PET DOG PLUTO STARRED IN FORTY-EIGHT OF HIS** own films, but also appeared along with Mickey Mouse and Donald Duck in many of their cartoons. The dog that would eventually evolve into Pluto made his debut as a bloodhound in the Mickey Mouse cartoon "The Chain Gang" in 1930. Later that year he appeared as Minnie Mouse's dog, Rover, in "The Picnic," and the following year he finally became Mickey's dog Pluto in "The Moose Hunt."

While his level of autonomy has varied over the years from obedient pet to independent agent (influenced at times by his own Angel-Pluto and Devil-Pluto), this pup's most enduring role is as Mickey's boon companion. Pluto continues to appear alongside his friends in current TV series and films.

WALT DISNEY'S PLUTO in *lend a paw*

with Dinah & Butch

Walt Disney's
PLUTO
THE PUP

No. 595

Walt Disney's
PLUTO

10¢

In 1942, Pluto headlined his first comic book, Dell's Large Feature Comic #7.

PLUTO BODY IS ABOUT FOUR HEADS LON[G] — STANDS ABOUT 3½ HEADS HIGH —

## CAREER

**FILM DEBUT:**
"The Chain Gang," 1930

**FILMOGRAPHY (HIGHLIGHTS):**
"The Picnic," 1930
"The Moose Hunt," 1931
"Fishin' Around," 1931
"Mickey's Orphans," 1931
  (Oscar nominee)
"Mickey's Revue," 1932
"The Klondike Kid," 1932
"Building a Building," 1933
  (Oscar nominee)
"Mickey's Pal Pluto," 1933
"Puppy Love," 1933
"Pluto's Judgment Day," 1935
"Pluto's Quin-Puplets," 1937
"The Pointer," 1939
  (Oscar nominee)
"Pluto, Junior," 1942
"The Army Mascot," 1942
"Private Pluto," 1943
"Springtime for Pluto," 1944
"Squatter's Rights," 1946
  (Oscar nominee)
"Pluto's Blue Note," 1947
  (Oscar nominee)
"Pluto's Heart Throb," 1950
"Pluto and the Gopher," 1950
"Food for Feudin'," 1950
"Camp Dog," 1950
Who Framed Roger Rabbit, 1988
  (cameo)
The Prince and the Pauper, 1990
Mickey Mouse Works, 1999
  (TV series)
Mickey's Once Upon
  A Christmas, 1999
Disney's House of Mouse, 2001
  (TV series)
Mickey's House of Villains, 2002
Mickey's Twice Upon
  A Christmas, 2004

**HONORS AND AWARDS:**
1941 Academy Award for
Lend a Paw

# FARM KIN

## THE FACTS

**NAME:** Clarabelle Cow

**ALSO CREDITED AS:** Carolyn Cow (in "Plane Crazy," 1929)

**VOICED BY:** Elvia Allman (1990); April Winchell (1999–present)

**SIGNIFICANT OTHERS:** Horace Horsecollar, Goofy

**SIBLINGS:** Sarabelle Cow (sister)

**OTHER CLOSE RELATIVES:** Bertie Cow (a.k.a. "Bertie the Jinx," a young cousin— first appeared as "Calfie" in the Sunday *Silly Symphony* comic strip, September 8, 1940); Boniface (cousin); Itsy-Betsy (niece); Miss Bovina (socialite aunt)

**DESCRIPTION:** Moosical, amoosing, somewhat moosterious, but still udderly cowptivating

**NOTABLE QUOTE:** "I'm so excited I could break down on all fours and moo!" ("The Great Orphanage Robbery," 1932)

**WORKS WELL WITH:** Horace Horsecollar, Clara Cluck, Minnie Mouse, Goofy

## CAREER

**FILM DEBUT:** "Alice on the Farm," 1926

**FILMOGRAPHY (HIGHLIGHTS):** "The Shindig," 1930 "Symphony Hour," 1942 *Mickey's Christmas Carol*, 1983 *Who Framed Roger Rabbit*, 1988 (cameo) *The Prince and the Pauper*, 1990 *Mickey Mouse Works*, 1999 (TV series) *Disney's House of Mouse*, 2001 (TV series) *The Three Musketeers*, 2004

## CLARABELLE COW

*It was in the comic strips that Horace and Clarabelle became an "item"— they announced their engagement in 1931.*

*For a brief time, in comic books and strips during the late 1960s, Clarabelle began dating Goofy! (During this time, Horace's whereabouts are unknown.)*

**LIKE MANY OF HOLLYWOOD'S CHARACTER ACTORS, CLARABELLE COW** started as an unnamed bit player. A bovine beauty of her likeness appeared in a pre–Mickey Mouse Disney film called "Alice on the Farm," and in 1929's "Plane Crazy," she appeared as "Carolyn." The name "Clarabelle Cow" did not materialize until the sixth Mickey cartoon, "The Shindig" (1930).

Clarabelle appeared in a handful of cartoons until "Symphony Hour" in 1942, after which she was not seen in a theatrical cartoon until *Mickey's Christmas Carol* (1983), *The Prince and the Pauper* (1990), and briefly in 1988's *Who Framed Roger Rabbit*. On modern television, she appeared in a few segments of *Mickey Mouse Works*, and she regularly performs as a gossip columnist in *Disney's House of Mouse*, where her catchphrase is, "Gossip is always true."

In her early days, Clarabelle's anatomy spawned a great many gags (owing largely to animator Ub Iwerks's fondness for udder jokes), until censorship pressure led to the addition of her modest skirt. Udder aside, Clarabelle never really claimed a place in viewers' hearts, and she remains, for the most part, a perennial extra.

*In Europe, especially in Italy, Clarabelle is still a big star in comic strips and stories.*

# HORACE HORSECOLLAR

**OFFICIAL** DOCUMENTS

**HORACE HORSECOLLAR IS ONE OF MICKEY MOUSE'S "FARM KIN" AND A** member of his social circle. He was originally presented as Mickey's plow horse, but he could walk upright on his hind legs, with his forelegs becoming gloved hands. (He and girlfriend Clarabelle share this uncanny ability.)

A versatile performer of modest depth, Horace sometimes plays a cheerful know-it-all. He was seen frequently in cartoon shorts from 1930 to 1932, less so afterward. Horace helped Mickey in comic strip sleuthing enterprises before Goofy assumed that role, but he appeared more commonly in gag situations. He was most recently seen on film in *The Prince and the Pauper* as Mickey's pompous tutor and on television in *Disney's House of Mouse* as a technician.

# CLARA CLUCK

*She may be related to the mother hen in "The Wise Little Hen" (the 1934 Silly Symphony that introduced Donald Duck)—there is more than a passing physical resemblance.*

**CLARA IS A CHICKEN BUILT LIKE A MIDDLE-AGED OPERA DIVA, WITH A** singing voice to match. She dresses for showbiz success in an outsized hat topped by an even more outsized feather.

The full-bosomed Madam Cluck fancies herself a professional actress, opera singer, and cellist. Aside from her many civic involvements, she also teaches at Huey, Dewey, and Louie's school. An occasional supporting player in Mickey Mouse cartoons, Clara appeared more frequently in comics as Daisy Duck's confidante. Her final appearance during the classic era of Disney shorts was in 1942's "Symphony Hour." Today, she sometimes appears on *Disney's House of Mouse* as part of Daisy's Chit Chat Society.

# PINOCCHIO

*Pinocchio premiered on February 7, 1940. The film was reissued theatrically in 1945, 1954, 1962, 1971, 1978, 1984, and 1992. It was released on home video in 1985, 1993, and 1999.*

## THE FACTS

**NAME:** Pinocchio

**VOICED BY:** Dickie Jones

**FATHER:** Geppetto

**SIBLINGS:** Several clocks and music boxes

**FRIENDS:** Figaro (kitten), Cleo (goldfish)

**CONSCIENCE:** Jiminy Cricket

**DESCRIPTION:** Eager to please, naive, innocent, and very gullible

**DOES NOT WORK WELL WITH:** Lampwick, Honest John (J. Worthington Foulfellow), Gideon (John's feline accomplice), Stromboli, cigars, whales

**SPECIAL NOTE:** You'll love working with him—no strings attached.

Monstro!
↓

ALTHOUGH PINOCCHIO PROMISED THE BLUE FAIRY HE'D BE GOOD, temptation can be a powerful force for any boy—even one made of wood. Curious and naive, Geppetto's "little woodenhead" has a solid thirst for adventure but a shaky sense of what's right and wrong, despite the persistent advice of his "official" conscience, Jiminy Cricket. An easy mark for the practiced con men of the world at large, Pinocchio had to beat temptation and learn to become brave, truthful, and, most of all, unselfish. Only when he proved himself deserving of the Blue Fairy's trust and his father's love did he become a real boy.

*Even as a puppet, Walt Disney's Pinocchio is more like a human boy than the marionette created by Italian author Carlo Collodi in 1880. Initially adhering closely to Collodi's original vision, Pinocchio's animators were not satisfied with the "wooden" appearance of their character.*

## FROM THE DESK OF
## WALT DISNEY

Technically and artistically [Pinocchio] was superior. It indicated that we had grown considerably as craftsmen.

### CAREER

**FILMOGRAPHY:**
Pinocchio, 1940

**HONORS AND AWARDS:**
1940 Academy Award for Best Original Score: Leigh Harline, Paul J. Smith, Ned Washington

1940 Academy Award for Best Song: "When You Wish Upon a Star" Leigh Harline (music), Ned Washington (lyrics)

1994 National Film Preservation Board, National Film Registry

PINOCCHIO

PINOCCHIO MARKS
© 1939
WALT DISNEY
PRODUCTIONS
Patented
U. S. Pat. No. 2821063

← with Geppetto

WHEN YOU WISH UPON A STAR

## Walt Disney's
## Pinocchio

WHEN YOU WISH UPON A STAR
GIVE A LITTLE WHISTLE
TURN ON THE OLD MUSIC BOX
LITTLE WOODEN HEAD
I'VE GOT NO STRINGS
HI - DIDDLE - DEE - DEE
(An Actors' Life For Me)
THREE CHEERS FOR ANYTHING

Lyric by Ned Washington
Music by Leigh Harline

© 1939 W.D.P.

PRICE 75¢
IN U.S.A.

**ALADDIN**

## THE FACTS

**NAME:** Aladdin

**ALIAS:** Prince Ali Ababwa

**VOICED BY:** Scott Weinger (speaking); Brad Kane (singing)

**SIGNIFICANT OTHER:** Princess Jasmine, daughter of the Sultan

**PARENTS:** None (orphan)

**PARTNER IN CRIME:** Abu, a small, long-tailed, fez-and-vest-wearing monkey (Abu fills many roles in Aladdin's life: roommate, accomplice, protector, and above all, pal)

**DESCRIPTION:** Good-hearted, carefree, and streetwise!

**WORKS WELL WITH:** Magic carpets, magic lamps, genies

**FAVORITE PHRASE:** "Do you trust me?"

**SPECIAL NOTE:** He's a diamond in the rough.

**ALADDIN IS A CLASSIC DISNEY HERO: BORN AND RAISED AMONG A DEN** of villains, yet brave, intelligent, steadfast, and quick-witted—even when he happens to be getting by as a street rat. Aladdin may not always have the most honest means of reaching an end, but he has a big heart and his schemes are always driven by good intentions.

Following a chance meeting with Princess Jasmine in the marketplace, Aladdin became determined to win her affections. With the help of Genie's magical powers, Aladdin found a way into the palace, but he gradually learned that honesty and integrity were the only ways into Jasmine's heart. Upon defeating Jafar and ridding the kingdom of his tyranny, Aladdin unselfishly used his third and final wish to set Genie free.

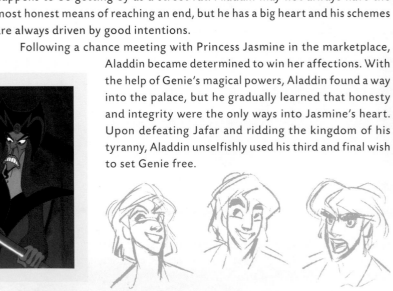

## CAREER

**FILMOGRAPHY:**
Aladdin, 1992
Aladdin: The Return
    of Jafar, 1994
Aladdin, 1994
    (TV series)
Aladdin and The King
    of Thieves, 1995

**HONORS AND AWARDS:**
1992 Academy Award for
Best Original Score:
Alan Menken

1992 Academy Award for Best
Song: "A Whole New World"
Alan Menken (music),
Tim Rice (lyrics)

1992 Academy Award nominee
for Best Song: "Friend Like Me"
Alan Menken (music),
Howard Ashman (lyrics)

1992 Academy Award nominee
for Sound: Terry Porter,
Mel Metcalfe, David J. Hudson,
Doc Kane

1992 Academy Award nominee
for Sound Effects Editing:
Mark Mangini

*In the first draft screenplay, Aladdin had three friends (named Babkak, Omar, and Kassim), a magic ring, and TWO genies.*

↑
*Romance in the air.*

# JASMINE

**VOICED BY:** Linda Larkin (speaking); Lea Salonga (singing)

**DESPITE THE FACT THAT THE LAWS OF AGRABAH DICTATED WHEN** Jasmine was to marry (before her rapidly approaching next birthday!), this headstrong princess refused to wed a man she didn't love. Feeling trapped by her station and her overprotective father, the Sultan, she ran away from the palace and met a kind and courageous street rat. Little did she know, he would ultimately be the one to win her heart.

*Whenever "Prince Ali" tells a lie, the plume on his hat falls and covers his face.*

## UNLIKELY HEROES ▶ SIMBA

### THE FACTS

**NAME:** Simba

**VOICED BY:** Jonathan Taylor Thomas (cub); Matthew Broderick (adult)

**SIGNIFICANT OTHER:** Nala

**FATHER:** Mufasa

**MOTHER:** Sarabi

**CLOSE RELATIVE:** Scar (uncle)

**DESCRIPTION:** Adventurous, good-hearted

**WORKS WELL WITH:** Meerkats, warthogs, mystical baboons

**DOES NOT WORK WELL WITH:** Wildebeests, hyenas

**CAREER GOAL:** To be king

Nala →

Several of Simba's friends' (and enemies') names are based on Swahili words:

Simba: Lion, Courageous Warrior

Shenzi: Barbarous, Uncouth, Uncivilized, Savage

Pumbaa: Ignorant, Lazy, Careless

Sarabi: Mirage

Rafiki: Comrade, Friend

**AS A CUB, SIMBA WAS TAUGHT TO RESPECT ALL CREATURES, GREAT** and small. Tragedy befell the young lion when a wildebeest stampede killed his father, the great King Mufasa. Blamed by his evil uncle, Scar, for the death, a scared and heartbroken Simba was convinced to run away.

So began the cub's journey from boyhood to manhood. Cast into exile, Simba learned to fend for himself with the help of meerkat Timon and warthog Pumbaa. The three enjoyed a lifestyle of *Hakuna Matata*—no worries, no cares—until Simba's old friend Nala appeared and pled for him to return and save the Pride Lands from Scar's reign of terror. With courage that honored his father's legacy, Simba sprung into action and took his rightful place in the circle of life as the new lion king. Honest and well-meaning, he serves his kingdom with an even paw.

It's all in the family with dad Mufasa (top) and Uncle Scar (above).

**FILMOGRAPHY:**
*The Lion King*, 1994
*Timon and Pumbaa*, 1995
    (TV series)
"The Lion King," 1997
    (Theatrical show)
*The Lion King 2:*
    *Simba's Pride*, 1998
*The Lion King 1½*, 2004

**HONORS AND AWARDS:**
1994 Academy Award for Best Original Score: Hans Zimmer

1994 Academy Award for Best Song: "Can You Feel the Love Tonight" Elton John (music), Tim Rice (lyrics)

1994 Academy Award nominee for Best Song: "Circle of Life" Elton John (music), Tim Rice (lyrics)

1994 Academy Award nominee for Best Song: "Hakuna Matata" Elton John (music), Tim Rice (lyrics)

"When I'm in charge . . ."

← with Rafiki

# POCAHONTAS

Pocahontas' real name was "Matoaca." Her father, Chief Powhatan, gave her the more familiar nickname "Pocahontas," which means "little mischief."

## THE FACTS

**NAME:** Pocahontas

**VOICED BY:** Irene Bedard (speaking); Judy Kuhn (singing)

**SIGNIFICANT OTHER:** John Smith

**FATHER:** Chief Powhatan

**OTHER CLOSE RELATIVES:** Grandmother Willow (not really her grandmother... nor really a willow)

**DESCRIPTION:** Spirited, brave, good-hearted

**WORKS WELL WITH:** Nakoma, Meeko (raccoon), Flit (hummingbird)

**DOES NOT WORK WELL WITH:** Kocoum, Governor Ratcliffe

**POCAHONTAS IS THE DAUGHTER OF CHIEF POWHATAN. RAISED IN** harmony with nature deep within the ancient forests of Virginia, she is an eternal optimist, always wondering where the next path or river will take her. Her father wishes that she would settle down and marry the serious and stern warrior Kocoum, but Pocahontas feels destiny holds a greater purpose for her.

When English settlers sailed across the Atlantic and arrived in her homeland, they saw the untouched wilderness as a "New World" full of riches ripe for the taking or taking over. Ever curious and a bit rebellious, Pocahontas ventured near the settlers' camp and stumbled upon a brave explorer named John Smith. Though inhibited by the boundaries of language and culture, their friendship grew into a love more powerful than social convention and more valuable than Governor Ratcliffe's gold.

**FILMOGRAPHY:**
*Pocahontas*, 1995
*Pocahontas II: Journey To A New World*, 1998

**HONORS AND AWARDS:**
1995 Academy Award for Best Original Musical or Comedy Score: Alan Menken (music, orchestral score), Stephen Schwartz (lyrics)

1995 Academy Award for Best Song: "Colors of the Wind" Alan Menken (music), Stephen Schwartz (lyrics)

# JOHN SMITH

**VOICED BY:** Mel Gibson

**A BRASH AND SPIRITED EXPLORER AND SCOUT FOR THE VIRGINIA** Company, Smith had been searching all his life for an unspoiled land when he arrived in the New World. Virginia turned out to be quite different than he could ever imagine, though. As his friendship with Pocahontas blossomed, Smith soon found his ideas of what is "wild" and what is "civilized" turned upside down.

*Over the years, storytellers have romanticized and embellished the known historical facts to the point where the story of Pocahontas has become a sort of Early-American Romeo and Juliet.*

29-55A.

# UNLIKELY HEROES ▶ QUASIMODO

## THE FACTS

**NAME:** Quasimodo

**VOICED BY:** Tom Hulce

**SIGNIFICANT OTHER:** Esmeralda

**CLOSE RELATIVES:** Judge Claude Frollo (guardian)

**DESCRIPTION:** Shy, curious, hopeful, loyal, loving, longing

**SPECIAL SKILLS:** Good with heights

**AS AN ORPHANED BABY, QUASIMODO (WHOSE NAME MEANS "PARTLY** formed") was left in the care of the sinister Frollo, who hid him in the bell tower of Notre Dame Cathedral, the highest point in all of Paris. There, Quasimodo grew into a young man whose job was to ring the cathedral's giant bells. He watched over the world, but the world never saw him.

Quasimodo's only friends were the birds and the stone gargoyles that live with him in the tower. They didn't care what he looked like, seeing the strength in his heart and the tenderness of his soul.

Because of his very limited experiences, Quasimodo is a bit like a child who just wants to go to the party but is having a real problem with his parents. Even though he has suffered vicious abuse and unfeeling mistreatment, his spirit remains indomitable.

The story of Quasimodo was inspired by Victor Hugo's visit to the cathedral of Notre Dame. There, incised deep into the stone, he saw the Latin word for "fate." He agonized over the origin of this curious and melancholy inscription, and was inspired to write the novel _Notre-Dame de Paris_ (1831).

*Esmeralda* ↓

**FILMOGRAPHY:**
*The Hunchback
of Notre Dame*, 1996
"De Glöckner von Notre Dame," 1999
(Theatrical show—Germany)
*The Hunchback
of Notre Dame II*, 2002

**HONORS AND AWARDS:**
1996 Academy Award for
Best Original Musical or
Comedy Score: Alan Menken
(music, orchestral score),
Stephen Schwartz (lyrics)

← With gargoyle
pals Victor, Hugo,
and Laverne.

# MULAN

## THE FACTS

**NAME:** Fa Mulan

**ETYMOLOGY:** Chinese, feminine (Mu = blossom; Lan = magnolia)

**ALIAS:** Ping (an Imperial Soldier)

**VOICED BY:** Ming-Na Wen (speaking); Lea Salonga (singing)

**SIGNIFICANT OTHER:** Li Shang, Captain of the Imperial Guard

**FATHER:** Fa Zhou

**MOTHER:** Fa Li

**OTHER CLOSE RELATIVES:** Grandmother Fa

**HORSE:** Khan

**DOG:** Little Brother

**DESCRIPTION:** Loyal, brave, heroic

**DOES NOT WORK WELL WITH:** Matchmakers, Shan Yu, ill-behaved dragons

**SPECIAL SKILLS:** Horses, explosives, athletics

The character of Mulan is based on an ancient Chinese legend, which is said to tell the exploits of a real-life girl warrior.

*as ping* ↓

In Asia, the story of Mulan is as well-known as the story of Cinderella is in Western culture.

**MULAN IS A MISFIT IN HER WORLD. EVERYTHING A PROPER YOUNG CHINESE** girl is supposed to be—graceful, demure, and quiet—she is not. But her personality made her well suited to a noble cause: when her homeland and family were threatened by an invasion of bloodthirsty Huns, Mulan ran away to join the army in her father's place. There, she learned that her courage, intelligence, and determination were traits that would ultimately empower her to bring honor to her family and herself.

## LITTLE BROTHER

**VOICED BY:** Chris Sanders

**SWEET, SPRIGHTLY, ABUNDANTLY** loyal, with unflagging energy, a wide smile, and a peppy bark. (And just a bit light in the smarts department.)

## CAREER

**FILMOGRAPHY:**
*Mulan*, 1998
*Mulan II*, 2004

**HONORS AND AWARDS:**
1998 Academy Award nominee for Original Musical or Comedy Score: Matthew Wilder (music), David Zippel (lyrics), Jerry Goldsmith (orchestral score)

*Mulan* won nine Annie Awards, including Outstanding Achievement in an Animated Theatrical Feature and Outstanding Individual Achievement for Directing in an Animated Feature Production.

*Mulan is braver and more independent than earlier Disney animated maidens were, and concerned with her family honor rather than finding a man!*

Mulan's noble steed, Khan
↓

## LI SHANG

**VOICED BY:** B. D. Wong (speaking); Donny Osmond (singing)

**A HARDY MILITARY LEADER WHO IS SENSITIVE IN NATURE,** Captain Shang is the noble and respected son of an esteemed military leader and hero. Strong both athletically and intellectually, he always does what is right, even if it puts his own life in jeopardy. At first his feelings for Mulan left him startled and confused, but eventually he came to appreciate the Emperor's knowing advice: "A girl like that doesn't come along every dynasty."

# STITCH

## THE FACTS

**NAME:** Experiment 626

**ALIAS:** Stitch

**VOICED BY:** Chris Sanders

**FATHER:** Mad scientist Dr. Jumba Jookiba

**SIBLINGS:** Experiments 001–625

**DESCRIPTION:** Alien powers inside a cuddly shell

**WORKS WELL WITH:** Lilo Pelekai, the Elvis Presley catalog

**DOES NOT WORK WELL WITH:** Nani Pelekai, David Kawena, Dr. Jumba Jookiba, Agent Pleakley, Captain Gantu, Mrs. Hasagawa, Cobra Bubbles, luau restaurants, fire, water, vehicles of any kind

**CATCH PHRASE:** "Meega nala Queesta!"

*The King lives!*

*The live-action monster footage that Stitch watches on a television is from Earth vs. the Spider (1958).*

**A MISCHIEF-MAKING CREATURE KNOWN** officially as "Experiment 626," Stitch is actually the result of an out-of-control genetic experiment. His powers include the ability to hide his extra limbs, antennae, and back spikes, giving him the appearance of a rather odd-looking dog.

Initial reactions to the creature were less than favorable. The Grand Councilwoman of the Galactic Federation sentenced his creator, a mad scientist named Jumba, to prison and decreed that 626 be transported to a distant desert asteroid. But before his sentence could be carried out, 626 stole a police cruiser and used its hyperdrive to reach Earth. Once there, he was immediately run

down by a sugar cane truck. He awoke in an animal shelter, where he "charmed" human girl Lilo into adopting him (at which point she dubbed him "Stitch").

Realizing that Lilo and her older sister, Nani, formed a perfect shield against his pursuers, Stitch welcomed the adoption and stuck like glue to his new family. In their warm presence, Stitch learned the concept of 'ohana (the Hawaiian term for family that means no one gets left behind or forgotten)—and realized that his new home was much more than just a handy hideout.

LILO & STITCH — M. VIGNAL 1999

## CAREER

**FILMOGRAPHY:**
*Lilo & Stitch*, 2002
*Stitch! The Movie*, 2003
*Lilo & Stitch: The Series*, 2003 (TV series)
*Lilo & Stitch 2: Stitch Has A Glitch*, 2005

**STITCH DEBUTED (INVADED, REALLY) IN A SERIES OF TRAILERS BASED ON SOME CLASSIC DISNEY MOVIES:**
*The Little Mermaid:* Stitch surfs a wave that crashes down on Ariel.

*Beauty and the Beast:* Stitch causes the chandelier to fall during the ballroom scene, nearly smashing Belle and the Beast.

*Aladdin:* Stitch steals Princess Jasmine from Aladdin during the "A Whole New World" magic carpet ride.

*The Lion King:* Stitch takes Simba's place on Pride Rock during the "Circle of Life" opening.

**HONORS AND AWARDS:**
2001 Academy Award nominee for Best Animated Feature: Chris Sanders

2002 Sarajevo Film Festival Audience Favorite

2003 Broadcast Film Critics Association Award nominee for Best Animated Feature

When Stitch awakes at the pound, the dogs shaking in fear in the corner of his cell are all the same breed that Lady encounters in her trip to the dog pound in the 1955 film *Lady and the Tramp*.

# COMICAL COWS

## THE FACTS

**NAME:** Mrs. Caloway

**VOICED BY:** Judi Dench

**DESCRIPTION:** Distinctive dialect; stiff upper lip; hat

**WORKS WELL WITH:** Pearl (a lady farmer), Abner (a farmhand), Jeb (a goat)

**SPECIAL NOTE:** Do not let Maggie take her hat.

## CAREER

**FILMOGRAPHY:**
*Home on the Range*, 2004

*Known for having performed in productions of The Milkmaid of Venice, Much A-Moo About Nothing, and Madame Bovinary.*

## MRS. CALOWAY

*Costuming: note the hat!*

"I'm not sure how a British cow got to Patch of Heaven, but I'm frightfully pleased she did."

—JUDI DENCH

**IN HER UNOFFICIAL ROLE AS BARNYARD** boss, Mrs. Caloway is a fastidious British cow with an air of authority and a stylish straw hat. She's very attached to the farm and less adventurous than the other cows, and also a bit more civilized and refined. Mrs. Caloway is very motherly and protective of Grace, and sees her as something of a project. But while she loves order and stability, when the chips are down this cautious cow can always be counted on to pitch in with her keen mind and sharp wit.

# MAGGIE

## THE FACTS

**NAME:** Maggie

**VOICED BY:** Roseanne Barr

**DESCRIPTION:** Sassy, brassy, and udderly gorgeous

**HONORS AND AWARDS:** Winner, Miss Bell Ringer Pageant; three-time winner of the Golden Udder Award; renowned as the original Happy Heifer

**DOES NOT WORK WELL WITH:** Alameda Slim, yodelers in general

## CAREER

**FILMOGRAPHY:**
*Home on the Range*, 2004

**MAGGIE IS A CUNNING AND CLEVER COW WITH A WINK IN HER EYE AND A** curl in her lip. Blessed with a snappy delivery, she brings a sense of fun with her jokes and one-liners, but she also has subtle timing and a great deadpan wit. Not exactly humble—in fact, quite bossy—but not without heart: Maggie rallied her fellow farm animals to take action and save their beloved Patch of Heaven.

# GRACE

## THE FACTS

**NAME:** Grace

**VOICED BY:** Jennifer Tilly

**DESCRIPTION:** Wide-eyed, with a penchant for New Age thinking

**WORKS WELL WITH:** Everyone

## CAREER

**FILMOGRAPHY:**
*Home on the Range*, 2004

*Appeared in the films American Cowpie and Bridget Jones's Dairy.*

### A THOUGHT FROM JENNIFER

"It's exciting that these cows are leaving the farm and going out into the big world. Everybody can identify with that: being out in a big open area where you don't really know what to expect, and where you have to survive with your ingenuity. The theme of *Home on the Range* is the value of friendship and how animals from all different types of farms can get along. Different breeds of cows can get along. It also shows that there's strength in numbers and that three heads are better than one."

—JENNIFER TILLY

**NEW-AGE SENSIBILITIES AND UNBRIDLED OPTIMISM DEFINE THIS TONE-** deaf young bovine who shuns confrontation. Grace is sort of the Switzerland of cows: the neutral peacemaker and diplomat. She also has a holistic saying for every circumstance. A bit on the green side, Grace exudes an air of innocence and beauty (except when she sings). As cows go, she's a very tie-dyed, aromatherapy-sniffing, candle-making, nature-loving, back-to-earth kind of gal.

# SNOW WHITE

## THE FACTS

**NAME:** Snow White

**ALSO KNOWN AS:** The little princess

**VOICED BY:** Adriana Caselotti

**LIVE-ACTION MODEL:** Marjorie Belcher (Marge Champion)

**SIGNIFICANT OTHER:** The Prince

**FATHER:** The King

**MOTHER:** Deceased

**STEPMOTHER, WICKED:** And how!

**DESCRIPTION:** Sweet, graceful, kindhearted, gentle, innocent

**WORKS WELL WITH:** Vertically challenged geologic engineers, forest fauna, gooseberry pies... even murderous huntsmen

**SPECIAL NOTE:** Stock dressing room with fruit, but NO APPLES!

*Snow White and the Seven Dwarfs, debuting in 1937, was the first full-length animated feature film to come out of the United States.*

↑
*Disneyland promotional poster*

**A PRINCESS OF NOBLE BIRTH, SNOW WHITE WAS FORCED INTO RAGS AS** a scullery maid by her jealous stepmother, the Queen. Blessed with an innocent's indomitable spirit, the fair maiden never lost faith that one day the wishing well would grant her a true love to come and take her away.

Of course, love comes with no guarantees. When a serenading young prince appeared at last to answer Snow White's dream, the evil Queen ordered her killed. Lucky for Snow White, the huntsman assassin could not bring himself to kill her and begged her to flee deep into the forest, never to return. Once again her innocence saved her, as the forest animals led her to the Seven Dwarfs' cottage, where she took on the role of their adopted mother (and won over even the woman-hating Grumpy... eventually).

The Queen, however, used the girl's naiveté against her, donning the guise of a helpless peddler hag to lure Snow White into biting a poisoned apple. As she fell into a sleeping death, Snow White's only hope was love's first kiss.

## CAREER

**FILMOGRAPHY:**
*Snow White and the*
   *Seven Dwarfs,* 1937

**HONORS AND AWARDS:**
A special Academy Award granted to the picture in 1939 consisted of one regular-sized award and seven smaller-sized awards.

Snow White was presented with her own star on the Hollywood Walk of Fame in 1987, in honor of the fiftieth anniversary of the release of *Snow White and the Seven Dwarfs*.

In 1989, *Snow White and the Seven Dwarfs* was the first animated feature to be selected for the National Film Registry.

*Snow White and the Seven Dwarfs* participated in a "handprint ceremony" in front of Grauman's Chinese Theatre in Hollywood on February 5, 2004.

33

## THE PRINCE

**VOICED BY:** Harry Stockwell

**A PERIPATETIC LAD OF NOBLE LINEAGE, THIS** prince on horseback happened across a tuneful princess named Snow White. His regal pipes combined in perfect harmony with hers, and his youthful zeal and passion created an instantaneous bond with her. His persistence and tenacity in finding his lost princess revealed his royal integrity.

OFF
DOCU

GRUMPY: (DISGUSTED) "HOW DO WE DO WHAT?"

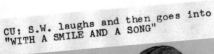

CU: S.W. laughs and then goes into
"WITH A SMILE AND A SONG"

# CINDERELLA

## THE FACTS

**NAME:** Cinderella

**VOICED BY:** Ilene Woods (1950); Jennifer Hale (2002)

**LIVE-ACTION MODEL:** Helene Stanley

**SIGNIFICANT OTHER:** Prince Charming

**FATHER:** Deceased

**MOTHER:** Deceased

**FAIRY GODMOTHER:** Alive and active

**SIBLINGS:** Stepsisters Anastasia and Drizella

**STEPMOTHER, WICKED:** Lady Tremaine

**DESCRIPTION:** Earnest, hard-working, clever, pretty, loyal

**WORKS WELL WITH:** Mice, birds, Bruno (a dog)

**SPECIAL NOTE:** Cleans up nicely

*More than a thousand versions of the Cinderella story have been recorded and cataloged worldwide. There is a famous version from Scotland called "Rashin Coatie," an Italian "Cat Cinderella," the Brothers Grimm's "Ash-Girl," even a Nigerian folktale called "The Maiden, the Frog, and the Chief's Son."*

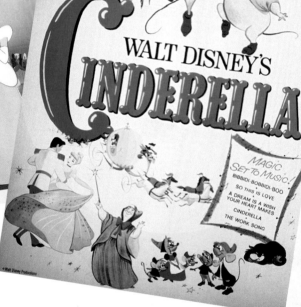

Bibbidi-Bobbidi-Boo... It's FUN! It's MAGIC!

WALT DISNEY'S CINDERELLA

MAGIC SET TO MUSIC!
BIBBIDI-BOBBIDI-BOO
SO THIS IS LOVE
A DREAM IS A WISH YOUR HEART MAKES
CINDERELLA
THE WORK SONG

*Note from wardrobe— loses shoes!*

**CINDERELLA IS BY NO MEANS A WEAK-WILLED SERVANT, CONTENT TO** let events flow around her. On the contrary, when an invitation to the royal ball was hand-delivered, she used everything short of physical force to persuade her cruel stepmother that she had every right to attend.

Still, it's been a "hard-knocks" life for this gal. For years, everyone ordered Cinderella around: her stepmother, her awful stepsisters—even the big clock in the church tower told her when to start each day of drudgery. But no matter how her family abused and humiliated her, she never stopped dreaming. For dreams are the wishes of Cinderella's heart, and, despite her sadness and hardships, her faith that her wishes of happiness would come true always remained unwavering. Eventually, her determination (and unusual taste in footwear) paid off royally.

**FILMOGRAPHY:**
Cinderella, 1950
Cinderella II: Dreams
    Come True, 2002

**HONORS AND AWARDS:**
1950 Academy Award nominee
for Best Scoring of a Musical
Picture: Oliver Wallace,
Paul J. Smith

1950 Academy Award nominee
for Best Song: "Bibbidi-
Bobbidi-Boo" Mack David,
Al Hoffman, and Jerry
Livingston (music and lyrics)

1950 Academy Award nominee
for Best Sound: Walt Disney
Studio Sound Department

1950 Winner, Special Prize,
Venice International
Film Festival

*The origin of the story many of us know today as Cinderella can actually be traced back to a 9th century tale from China.*

# PRINCE CHARMING

**VOICED BY:** William Phipps (speaking); Mike Douglas (singing)

**A HANDSOME AND SENSITIVE YOUNG MAN WITH A LOVELY SINGING** voice, this royal issue has extremely high standards for female companionship. He is dogged and persistent in pursuit of his princess-to-be once he has discovered her, but like many of royal state, leaves the actual search to his underlings.

# AURORA

*The tale of "The Sleeping Beauty" dates back to a 1528 Arthurian romance.*

## THE FACTS

**NAME:** Aurora

**ALIAS:** Briar Rose

**VOICED BY:** Mary Costa

**LIVE-ACTION MODEL:**
Helene Stanley

**SIGNIFICANT OTHER:**
Prince Phillip

**FATHER:** King Stefan

**MOTHER:** The Queen

**SIBLINGS:** None

**DESCRIPTION:** Graceful,
beautiful, and loved by
all who know her

**SPECIAL NOTE:** Needs
wake-up service

*The famous Italian storyteller Giambattista Basile wrote his version of the story, called "Sun, Moon, and Talia," in 1636.*

**BETROTHED AT BIRTH TO PRINCE PHILLIP (THE SON OF A NEIGHBORING** king) at her first court appearance, the infant Aurora was blessed with the gifts of beauty and song by the good fairies of the kingdom. But fate's icy hand brought an uninvited guest, the evil fairy Maleficent, who cursed Aurora to die by the prick of a spinning wheel's spindle before the sun set on her sixteenth birthday. Struggling to prevent this catastrophe, the good fairies changed the curse from death to eternal sleep until she received her true love's kiss and hid the princess in a secluded cottage in a glen. Aurora blossomed into a lovely but lonely young woman, unaware of her real name and birthright.

Playacting with the forest animals at what it might be like to meet a prince, Aurora, by this time called Briar Rose, met

## CAREER

**FILMOGRAPHY:**
Sleeping Beauty, 1959

*Charles Perrault published his famous version of "Sleeping Beauty" in his 1697 History of Tales from Times Past.*

# PRINCE PHILLIP

**VOICED BY:** Bill Shirley

**LESS DULL AND HUMORLESS THAN OTHER ROYAL PROGENY,** Phillip is a proficient horseman and enjoys the company of his steed, Samson. His sense of humor (inherited from his jovial father, King Hubert) masks a steely resolve and a brave spirit.

*After Perrault, the Brothers Grimm wrote their version, called "Little Briar-Rose," in 1812.*

a very real young man. Although neither of them knew the other's identity, the couple fell in love at first sight. Hence, when the good fairies revealed Aurora's birthright to her, instead of joy, an awful sadness came over her—for she believed she must sacrifice her true love to the "right and royal duty" of marrying some stranger, this "Prince Phillip." Just as she was about to discover that the two were one and the same, she was stricken by Maleficent's terrible curse. All seemed lost but for one glimmer of hope: the age-old truth that only true love's kiss can wake a sleeping beauty from eternal slumber.

# ARIEL

## THE FACTS

**NAME:** Ariel

**VOICED BY:** Jodi Benson

**LIVE-ACTION MODEL:**
Sherri Stoner

**SIGNIFICANT OTHER:**
Prince Eric

**FATHER:** King Triton

**MOTHER:** Deceased

**SIBLINGS:** Six sisters (Aquatta, Andrina, Arista, Adella, Alana, Attina)

**DESCRIPTION:** Confident, curious, adventurous; gifted with a beautiful voice

**WORKS WELL WITH:** Flounders, crabs, seagulls

**DOES NOT WORK WELL WITH:** Punctuality, eels, sea witches

**CO-STAR COMMENT:** "Somebody's got to nail that girl's fin to the floor!" (Sebastian)

**HOBBIES:** Exploring shipwrecks, collecting human artifacts

CONFIDENTIAL

**RED-HAIRED MERMAID ARIEL IS A TEENAGE GIRL IN THE PROCESS** of becoming a beautiful young woman. Though constantly warned by her father, King Triton, that humans are dangerous, this stubborn and precocious mermaid secretly collects human artifacts and often fantasizes about walking and dancing on land.

After rescuing the handsome Prince Eric from a shipwreck, Ariel resolved to become part of the human world—no matter the cost. Blinded by love, she willingly struck a bargain with the evil sea witch, Ursula, to become human for three days, using her beautiful voice as payment. Ursula's contract stipulated that Eric had to kiss Ariel before the sun set on the third day or she would become a part of the sea witch's garden of slaves. With the help of Ariel's friends Sebastian, Flounder, and Scuttle, Ursula was defeated and true love won the day.

Danish author Hans Christian Andersen wrote the original _The Little Mermaid_, in which he transformed the mermaid, usually thought of by sailors as a dangerous enchantress, into a symbol of the spirit of the sea.

**FILMOGRAPHY:**
The Little Mermaid, 1989
The Little Mermaid, 1992–1994
   (TV series)
The Little Mermaid II:
   Return to the Sea, 2000

**HONORS AND AWARDS:**
1989 Academy Award for
Original Score: Alan Menken

1989 Academy Award for
Best Song: "Under the Sea"
Alan Menken (music), Howard
Ashman (lyrics)

1989 Academy Award nominee
for Best Song: "Kiss the Girl"
Alan Menken (music), Howard
Ashman (lyrics)

1989 Golden Globe Award nominee
for Best Motion Picture, Comedy
or Musical

# PRINCE ERIC

**VOICED BY:** Christopher Daniel Barnes

**DOG:** Max

**TUTOR:** Grimsby

**ERIC IS THE YOUNG AND HANDSOME MONARCH OF A SMALL** and picturesque seaside kingdom. Despite pressure from Grimsby to get married, Eric is resolute in his desire to find true love with the right girl.

Haunted by Ariel's voice after a fleeting encounter, Eric was disappointed to discover that the beautiful girl who washed up on his beach was unable to speak. But when Ursula's evil plot was revealed, his bravery and love for Ariel saved two kingdoms, land and sea, from a terrible fate.

# BELLE

## THE FACTS

**NAME:** Belle

**VOICED BY:** Paige O'Hara

**LIVE-ACTION MODEL:**
Sherri Stoner

**SIGNIFICANT OTHER:**
Beast

**FATHER:** Maurice
(an inventor)

**MOTHER:** Deceased

**HORSE:** Phillipe

**DESCRIPTION:** Smart,
sassy, independent,
assertive, determined

**WORKS WELL WITH:**
Inanimate objects

**DOES NOT WORK WELL WITH:**
Superficial suitors

**CO-STAR COMMENT:** "Belle
always has her head in a book.
She should be paying attention
to more important things—
like me!" (Gaston)

**HOBBIES:** Reading,
pruning roses

*Walt Disney himself tried twice to adapt Beauty and the Beast as an animated feature. He and his team could never overcome key story obstacles.*

## CAREER

**FILMOGRAPHY:**
*Beauty and the Beast*, 1991
"Beauty and the Beast," 1994
  (Theatrical show)
*Beauty and the Beast:
  The Enchanted Christmas*, 1997
*Beauty and the Beast:
  Belle's Magical World*, 1998

**HONORS AND AWARDS
(HIGHLIGHTS):**
1991 Academy Award for
Best Song: "Beauty and the
Beast" Alan Menken (music),
Howard Ashman (lyrics)

1991 Academy Award for Best
Original Score: Alan Menken

1991 Academy Award nominee
for Best Picture: Don Hahn
(producer)

**A DEEP LOVE OF READING HAS INSPIRED IN BELLE THE LONGING FOR A** life of adventure and excitement—not exactly the typical dreams of a small-town girl whose peers don't aspire to anything more than marrying a narcissistic hunk like Gaston.

Still, adventure was the last thing on her mind when she rode her horse, Phillipe, into the forest to find her beloved father, who had gone missing. She soon found herself making a terrible bargain with a pitiless monster, a beast that held her father captive. Voluntarily taking her father's place, Belle became a prisoner in a castle filled with enchanted objects and mysterious corridors. Though Beast was short-tempered and difficult at first, Belle saw something inside him that he was unable to see himself. And, with perseverance and kindness, she was able to prove to him that love sees past appearances.

*Chip is the only object in the Beast's castle to mention Belle by name. All of the other objects refer to her as "mademoiselle," "she," "the girl," and so forth.*

# ROYALTY ▶ BEAST

## THE FACTS

**NAME:** Beast

**VOICED BY:** Robby Benson

**SIGNIFICANT OTHER:** Belle

**DESCRIPTION:** Hot-tempered and monstrous-looking; vulnerable and gentle at the core

← great dancers

Versions of Belle and the Beast's tale—a beautiful girl in love with a beastly suitor—exist all over the world. There is the Greek myth of Cupid and Psyche, _Cyrano de Bergerac,_ _The Hunchback of Notre Dame,_ and even _King Kong._

**IN ACTUALITY, THE BEAST IS A PRINCE TRANSFORMED BY AN ENCHANTMENT** because he was without love in his heart. The fearful spell that rendered him terrifying could only be broken when he learned to love—and earned the love of another. But a beast tends to make a lousy first impression, and as the years ticked by, all seemed hopeless... until fate brought Belle into his home. Angry and despairing due to his long enchantment, the Beast tried to capture her heart with fear, the only way the gruff prince knew how to react. But slowly, through Belle's courage and compassion, he began to unlock the secrets of his own heart and discovered that even a beast can be loved.

## ROYALTY ▶ KUZCO

### THE FACTS

**NAME:** Kuzco

**VOICED BY:** David Spade

**SIGNIFICANT OTHER:** For Kuzco there is no other!

**DESCRIPTION:** Arrogant, egocentric, juvenile

**WORKS WELL WITH:** Nobody, really...

**DOES NOT WORK WELL WITH:** Everyone, but especially aged sorceresses, their hunky henchmen, llamas

**CATCH PHRASE:** "It's all about ME."

Kuzco was named after the ancient capital of the Incas, Cuzco (pronounced the same).

**WITH A "GROOVE" TO MAINTAIN AND A KINGDOM TO RUN, KUZCO IS ONE** hip cat. In fact, he may well be the hippest dude in creation. He's the sovereign lord of the nation and the product of generations of selective breeding. Long on confidence and swagger, if he had his way the entire world would spin around his every whim. Too bad his shifty ex-administrator Yzma and her right-hand man, Kronk, had designs on his throne....

After Yzma turned Kuzco into a llama in an attempt to seize power, Kuzco was thrown into the mix with a lowly but lovable peasant named Pacha. Although they didn't quite hit it off at first, their growing friendship helped the arrogant emperor learn that magnanimity is more rewarding than selfishness.

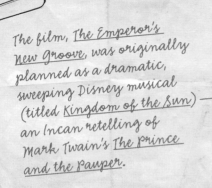

The film, *The Emperor's New Groove*, was originally planned as a dramatic, sweeping Disney musical (titled *Kingdom of the Sun*) — an Incan retelling of Mark Twain's *The Prince and the Pauper*.

Kuzco & Pacha in a tight fix ↓

## CAREER

**FILMOGRAPHY:**
*The Emperor's New Groove*, 2000
*Kronk's New Groove*, 2005
*The Emperor's New School*, 2006 (TV series)

**HONORS AND AWARDS:**
2001 Blockbuster Entertainment Award for Favorite Family Film

2001 Annie Award for Outstanding Individual Achievement for Character Animation: Dale Baer

2001 Annie Award for Outstanding Individual Achievement for Voice Acting by a Female Performer in an Animated Feature Production: Eartha Kitt

2001 Annie Award for Outstanding Individual Achievement for a Song in an Animated Production: David Hartley ("Perfect World")

# JIMINY CRICKET

## THE FACTS

**NAME:** Jiminy Cricket

**VOICED BY:**
Cliff Edwards (1940–1971);
Eddie Carroll (1975–present)

**DESCRIPTION:** Friendly, curious, concerned, grateful

**OCCUPATION:** Conscience

**CO-STAR COMMENT:**
"He's no fool." (J. Worthington Foulfellow)

**FAVORITE PHRASES:** "Give a little whistle" "I'm no fool" "That's the nature of things"

Ward Kimball developed the character design of Jiminy Cricket. Walt saw in the Cricket an opportunity to create a "familiar," a character with whom audiences could identify, and whose role as conscience would soften the amorality of the title character. Kimball refined initial, buglike designs into a character that looks more like a little man than an insect (more "Jiminy" than "Cricket").

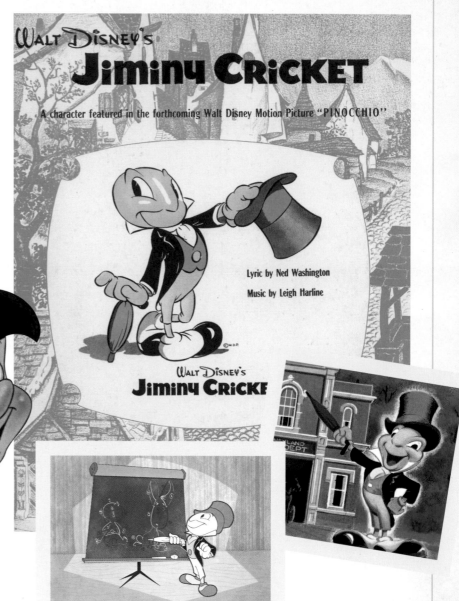

**WALT DISNEY'S Jiminy Cricket**

A character featured in the forthcoming Walt Disney Motion Picture "PINOCCHIO"

Lyric by Ned Washington

Music by Leigh Harline

WALT DISNEY'S Jiminy Cricke

**JIMINY MAY BE SMALL, BUT HE'S FAR FROM YOUR AVERAGE CRICKET. HE** can turn an umbrella into a parachute and looks great in a top hat and spats. He carries a mean tune, as well as a nearly inexhaustible supply of home-brewed common sense. It's no wonder he was chosen by the Blue Fairy to be Pinocchio's official conscience. (Unfortunately for Jiminy, it was only after he blushingly accepted his appointment as "Lord High Keeper of the Knowledge of Right and Wrong, Counselor in Moments of Temptation, and Guide along the Straight and Narrow Path," that he realized what a job he'd gotten himself into.)

Like any conscience, Jiminy is occasionally late on the job and frequently ignored even when he is around. Fortunately, Jiminy is nothing if not persistent, and he eventually succeeded in steering Pinocchio back to the right path.

**FILMOGRAPHY:**

**FEATURES / FEATURETTES:**
*Pinocchio*, 1940
*Fun and Fancy Free*, 1947
*Mickey's Christmas Carol*, 1983
 (Oscar nominee)

**TELEVISION (HIGHLIGHTS):**
"I'm No Fool" Series, 1950s
 (for *The Mickey Mouse Club*)
"Nature of Things" Series, 1950s
 (for *The Mickey Mouse Club*)
"On Vacation," 1956
"This Is Your Life,
 Donald Duck," 1960
"From All of Us to All of You,"
 1960s–1970s

**HONORS AND AWARDS:**
The Disney signature anthem,
"When You Wish Upon a Star,"
was sung by Jiminy Cricket in
*Pinocchio*, and won the Academy
Award for Best Song.

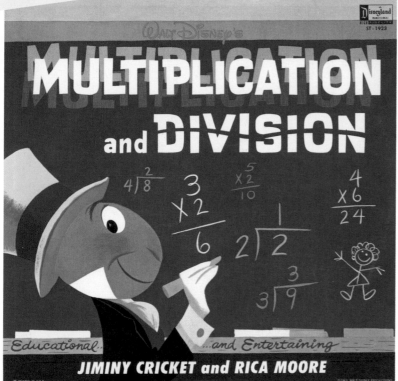

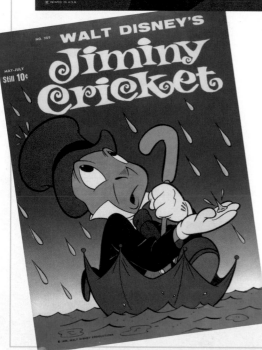

Jiminy was the first
Disney feature
character to speak
directly to the audience.
This set the tone for his
going on to become
one of Disney's premier
emcees, educators,
and storytellers, both
on TV and in
educational media.

*Figaro and Cleo →*

# JOSÉ CARIOCA

*In his homeland of Brazil, José is a comic book superstar. He headlined his first comic book there in 1961, and has been a Brazilian Disney star ever since.*

## THE FACTS

**NAME:** José Carioca

**VOICED BY:**
José Oliveira (1943);
Rob Paulsen (current)

**DESCRIPTION:** Mix one part bouncy beat, two parts tropical tempo, and three parts Rio romance, and you've got a melody shaken purely for fun!

## CAREER

**FILMOGRAPHY:**
*Saludos Amigos*, 1943
*The Three Caballeros*, 1945
*Melody Time*, 1948
   ("Blame it on the
   Samba" segment)
*Mickey Mouse Works*, 1999
   (TV series)
*Disney's House of Mouse*, 2001
   (TV series)

*José made his actual first appearance in the comics. On October 11, 1942, the <u>Silly Symphonies</u> comic strip began running his adventures. His film debut came on February 6, 1943.*

© WALT DISNEY

**OFFICIAL DOCUMENTS**

From <u>Don Markstein's Toonpedia</u>™

"...[José Carioca] became so popular in Brazil in the early 1960s [that] the publisher had local production artists erase Donald Duck and Mickey Mouse from proofs of American comics and draw José Carioca in their place. This resulted in a couple of nephews, Zico and Zeca, to take the place of the nephews already in the stories. In more recent years, the Brazilian version has even become a superhero, *Morcego Verde* (The Green Bat)."

**IN BRAZILIAN LINGO, A CARIOCA IS A RIO DE JANEIRO AFICIONADO; AND** José is "Joseph" in Spanish. So, loosely translated, José Carioca means "Joe from Rio." And Rio is where José the parrot was introduced in "Aquarela do Brasil," the fourth segment of *Saludos Amigos*.

José Carioca is a playboy parrot, and if there's one thing he loves more than the ladies, it's his native land of Brazil. So it was his pleasure to become Donald Duck's suave tour guide. Whether they were visiting the seaside village of Baìa or the capital city, Rio de Janeiro, he was determined to show Donald that his land's greatest treasure might just be the samba.

*José Oliveira and Clarence Nash vocally reprised their roles as José Carioca and Donald Duck in guest-star appearances on the original <u>Mickey Mouse Club</u> television show (1955–1958) and <u>Walt Disney Presents</u>.*

# PANCHITO

## THE FACTS

**NAME:** Panchito Romero Miguel Junipero Francisco Quintero Gonzales

**ALSO KNOWN AS:** Panchito Pistoles; Pancho el Charro

**VOICED BY:** Joaquin Garay (1945); Carlos Alazraqui (current)

**SIGNIFICANT OTHER:** Margarita (girlfriend)

**HORSE:** Señor Martinez

**DESCRIPTION:** Energetic, enthusiastic, loud

## CAREER

**FILMOGRAPHY:**
*The Three Caballeros*, 1945
*Disney's House of Mouse*, 2001
  (TV series)

Panchito made his animated debut in *The Three Caballeros*, released in the U.S. on February 3, 1945, but like José Carioca, his actual first appearance was in a comic book: *Walt Disney's Comics & Stories #35* (August 1943), where he appeared in a text story about him and Donald Duck.

**"IIIEEEE-AH-AH!" COMES THE CRY OF PANCHITO, THE UNMISTAKABLE** *pollo pistolero Mexicano* (pistol-packing chicken from Mexico). Brightly dressed in reddish-brown plumage, vermillion clothing with yellow highlights, and a picturesque sombrero, this raucous caballero has a habit of punctuating everything he says with pistol fire—and firing his pistols even when he's not saying anything.

The third of the Three Caballeros, he once treated pals Donald Duck and José Carioca to a trip through Mexico on his magic *serape* (Mexican blanket). Proud of his beloved country, he made the mistake of bringing them to Acapulco Beach, where Donald went gaga for the local bathing beauties. Luckily, Panchito and his blanket swooped down to carry the rambunctious duck away before he could get too... carried away.

## SIDEKICKS ▶ BALOO

### THE FACTS

**NAME:** Baloo

**ETYMOLOGY:** Baloo comes from the Hindi word for "bear"

**VOICED BY:**
Phil Harris (1967);
Ed Gilbert (1990);
John Goodman (2003)

**WORKS WELL WITH:** Mowgli, Colonel Hathi, Bagheera

**DOES NOT PAIR WELL WITH:** Kaa, King Louie, Shere Khan

**FACTOID:** "Baloo" is the pen name of cartoonist Rex F. May

### CAREER

**FILMOGRAPHY:**
*The Jungle Book*, 1967
*TaleSpin*, 1990
   (TV series)
*Jungle Cubs*, 1996
   (TV series)
*The Jungle Book 2*, 2003

**AN EASYGOING "JUNGLE BUM," BALOO IS A BIG, LOVABLE BEAR. AT** first glance, he might seem an unlikely mentor, but his jovial nature makes him well suited to befriending a child. He and his reluctant jungle companion, Bagheera, shared the responsibility for taking "man-cub" Mowgli to the man-village and out of harm's way in the jungle, where villainous Shere Khan is always on the prowl.

Baloo also shares with Bagheera deep roots in literature. From the 1930s on, Walt Disney was always on the lookout for stories to translate into the animated feature medium. Rudyard Kipling's 1894 classic *The Jungle Book* and its 1895 sequel fascinated him for decades. The tenacious Walt finally acquired the film rights in 1962 and immediately told members of his key creative team, including director Wolfgang Reitherman and composers Richard M. and Robert B. Sherman, to *ignore* the classic book!

Walt was more interested in the vivid characters and exotic settings of Kipling than the storyline itself. He encouraged his creative team to take the characters delineated in the book—Baloo, along with Bagheera and even Mowgli himself—and develop them in the Disney fashion, which led to the characters fans recognize from *The Jungle Book* films and TV series.

# BAGHEERA

## THE FACTS

**NAME:** Bagheera

**ETYMOLOGY:** Bagheera means "panther" in Hindi

**VOICED BY:**
Sebastian Cabot (1967);
Bob Joles (2003)

**WORKS WELL WITH:** Mowgli, Colonel Hathi, Baloo

**DOES NOT PAIR WELL WITH:** Kaa, King Louie, Shere Khan

## CAREER

**FILMOGRAPHY:**
*The Jungle Book,* 1967
*Jungle Cubs,* 1996
   (TV series)
*The Jungle Book 2,* 2003

**BAGHEERA IS A SLEEK AND WELL-MANNERED** black panther who spends most of his jungle time with Baloo. When shouldering responsibility for young Mowgli, Bagheera acted as a prim but sympathetic authority figure, providing the voice of reason that balanced out Baloo's fun-loving but occasionally foolish "parenting" style.

# SEBASTIAN

## THE FACTS

**NAME:** Horatio Felonious Ignatious Crustaceous Sebastian

**VOICED BY:** Samuel E. Wright

**DESCRIPTION:** Prim, dignified, intellectual, with a personality far larger than his carriage

## CAREER

**FILMOGRAPHY:**
*The Little Mermaid*, 1989
*The Little Mermaid*, 1992–1994
  (TV series)
*The Little Mermaid II:*
  *Return to the Sea*, 2000

STUDIO CIRCULATION ONLY

**SEBASTIAN IS A CRUSTACEAN COMPOSER AND LOYAL MUSICIAN TO THE** court of King Triton who found himself assigned as a guardian and *de facto* conscience of the rebellious teenage mer-princess Ariel. Her lack of discipline and desire for interaction with the human world proved to be a frustrating counterpoint to Sebastian's melody of conventionality; in the end, though, the two composed a harmonious duet.

# FLOUNDER, SCUTTLE

## THE FACTS

**NAME:** Flounder

**ETYMOLOGICAL NOTE:** Although the term "flounder" refers to marine flatfishes, its alternate (and fitting) meaning is "to proceed in an unsteady, faltering manner; to bumble."

**VOICED BY:**
Jason Marin (1989);
Bradley Pierce (1992–1994);
Edan Gross (1992)

## CAREER

**FILMOGRAPHY:**
*The Little Mermaid*, 1989
*The Little Mermaid*, 1992–1994
  (TV series)
*The Little Mermaid II:*
  *Return to the Sea*, 2000

## THE FACTS

**NAME:** Scuttle

**ETYMOLOGICAL NOTES:**
A "scuttle" is a small opening in the hull of a ship. Informally, it means to scrap or discard.

"Scuttlebutt" is a cask on a ship used to hold drinking water. Apropos to this seagull, it also means gossip or sensational talk about others.

**VOICED BY:** Buddy Hackett

**DESCRIPTION:** Kooky, chatty, scruffy; an "avian egghead" of sorts

## CAREER

**FILMOGRAPHY:**
*The Little Mermaid*, 1989
*The Little Mermaid*, 1992–1994
  (TV series)
*The Little Mermaid II:*
  *Return to the Sea*, 2000

## FLOUNDER

**FLOUNDER IS THE FISH NEXT DOOR, AN EAGER AND LOYAL EVER-READY** pal and boon companion always prepared for the next big adventure (and occasional *mis*adventure). His naiveté often results in Ariel leading him along into places and situations his own anxiety and common sense might never allow—but he's never really any the worse for it.

## SCUTTLE

**SCUTTLE IS AN UNPERTURBED AND UNFLAPPABLE SEAGULL, AS** comfortable in the air as he is skipping across the ocean waves. He shares Ariel's fascination with relics and artifacts of the human world. Unlike Ariel, though, Scuttle is a vast repository of information about humans and their habits, from snarfblatt etiquette to the proper employment of a dinglehopper.

# LUMIERE

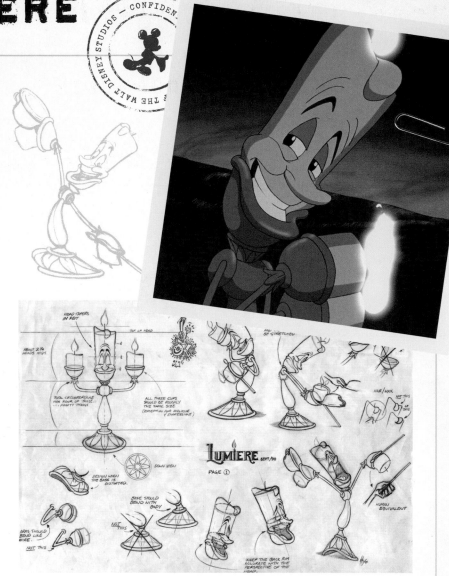

## THE FACTS

**NAME:** Lumiere

**VOICED BY:** Jerry Orbach

**SIGNIFICANT OTHER:** A flirtatious feather-duster named Babette is a particular sweetheart of this fired-up fellow

**DESCRIPTION:** Suave, debonair, sophisticated

**CO-STAR COMMENT:** "Watch out—I was burnt by him before." (Babette)

## CAREER

**FILMOGRAPHY:**
*Beauty and the Beast*, 1991
"*Beauty and the Beast*," 1994
   (Theatrical show)
*Beauty and the Beast:*
   *The Enchanted Christmas*, 1997
*Beauty and the Beast:*
   *Belle's Magical World*, 1998

**THE PRINCE'S VALET AND THE *DE FACTO* MAITRE D' OF THE HOUSE, LUMIERE** is also a gastronome, a romantic, and even quite a polished *artiste du cabaret*. When the sorceress enchanted the castle, Lumiere became a candelabra, in keeping with his illuminating charm and glowing personality. Whether mortal or magical, his amorous flair remains ever-alight.

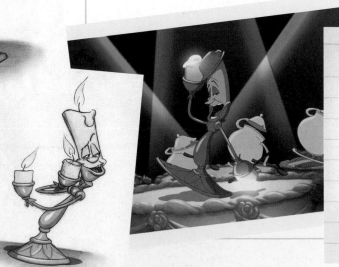

Louis Lumiére and his brother Auguste, sons of Antoine Lumiére, the photography pioneer, invented a camera/projector called the cinematograph—and were instrumental in the development of moving pictures as a popular art form.

# COGSWORTH, MRS. POTTS

## COGSWORTH

### THE FACTS

**NAME:** Cogsworth

**VOICED BY:** David Ogden Stiers

**DESCRIPTION:** Precise, punctual, and efficient (though wound a little tight)

**DOES NOT WORK WELL WITH:** His colleague, Lumiere (whose *joie de vivre* is a constant annoyance)

### CAREER

**FILMOGRAPHY:**
*Beauty and the Beast*, 1991
"Beauty and the Beast," 1994
   (Theatrical show)
*Beauty and the Beast:*
   *The Enchanted Christmas*, 1997
*Beauty and the Beast:*
   *Belle's Magical World*, 1998

**ONCE THE BUTLER OF THE BEAST'S CASTLE, COGSWORTH IS CHARGED** with keeping things orderly, well-organized, and running on schedule. The satisfaction of his master and the efficiency of the household are his primary goals. Cogsworth does not run well with surprises and spontaneity; his clockwork competence and calculable predictability make it unsurprising that he was transformed into a mantel clock when the big enchantment was cast.

## MRS. POTTS

*Chip* →

### THE FACTS

**NAME:** Mrs. Potts

**VOICED BY:** Angela Lansbury

**OTHER CLOSE RELATIVES:** Chip (son...and teacup)

**DESCRIPTION:** Motherly, comforting, reassuring, level-headed—and just a bit romantic

**WORKS WELL WITH:** Everyone, even the most unsympathetic characters in the most unpleasant situations

### CAREER

**FILMOGRAPHY:**
*Beauty and the Beast*, 1991
"Beauty and the Beast," 1994
   (Theatrical show)
*Beauty and the Beast:*
   *The Enchanted Christmas*, 1997
*Beauty and the Beast:*
   *Belle's Magical World*, 1998

**MRS. POTTS IS THE HOUSEKEEPER OF THE CASTLE. AN EFFICIENT AND** cozy sort of household director, she is also something of a surrogate mother and voice of gentle conscience to the hotheaded master of the manor. The enchantment transformed her into a warm and cheering teapot, always filled to overflowing with soothing sympathy and wholesome common sense.

# TIMON

*"Hakuna matata" is a Swahili saying meaning "no worries." Literally translated, it means "There are no concerns here."*

## THE FACTS

**NAME:** Timon

**VOICED BY:** Nathan Lane

**DESCRIPTION:** Carefree loafer

**SPECIAL NOTE:** Watch out for wisecracks

## CAREER

**FILMOGRAPHY:**

*The Lion King*, 1994

*Timon and Pumbaa*, 1995
   (TV series)

"The Lion King," 1997
   (Theatrical show)

*The Lion King 2:
   Simba's Pride*, 1998

*The Lion King 1½*, 2004

## DESCRIPTION

**ONCE A MEMBER OF A LARGE AND THRIVING COLONY OF MEERKATS FAR** from Pride Rock, Timon was never in his element digging and guarding the holes as a unit with his fellow meerkats. One too many incidents in which his daydreaming and misplaced ingenuity brought real danger down upon the colony caused his Uncle Max to kick him out of the clan. Despite protests from his Ma, Timon set out to seek adventure and fulfillment out in the greater world. After a chance meeting with the mystic mandrill Rafiki, who taught him the feel-good philosophy of *Hakuna Matata*, Timon met an unlikely partner in the blundering warthog Pumbaa, with whom he sought the perfect responsibility-free home. They found it in the jungle that lies across the desert from the Pride Lands, and a steady diet of multicolored bugs kept Timon and Pumbaa well fed, with no need to hunt or forage.

*The meerkat, or suricate, is a small mammal and a member of the mongoose family. It inhabits all parts of the Kalahari Desert in southern Africa. A group of meerkats is called a "mob" or "gang."*

# PUMBAA

← *Pumbaa means "lazy" or "careless" in Swahili.*

## THE FACTS

**NAME:** Pumbaa

**VOICED BY:** Ernie Sabella

**DESCRIPTION:** Carefree loafer

**SPECIAL NOTE:** Keep plenty of air freshener around

**CO-STAR COMMENT:**
"With Pumbaa, everything's gas." (Timon)

## CAREER

**FILMOGRAPHY:**
The Lion King, 1994
Timon and Pumbaa, 1995
   (TV series)
"The Lion King," 1997
   (Theatrical show)
The Lion King 2:
   Simba's Pride, 1998
The Lion King 1½, 2004

## DESCRIPTION

CONFIDENTIAL

0885  9       46

The warthog (Phacochoerus africanus) is a wild member of the pig family that lives in Africa. Warthogs are identifiable by the two pairs of tusks protruding from their mouth, which are used as weapons against predators. Warthogs range in size from three to five feet in length and weigh between 110 and 330 pounds.

**AMIABLE PUMBAA IS CURSED WITH THE ULTIMATE IN SOCIAL STIGMA:** uncontrollable flatulence. His family background is a mystery, but his story from the point when he met Timon says all there is to say about his sad exile from the company of those who can't abide his smell. Dull-witted but packed with common sense, Pumbaa uncomplainingly shoulders the burdens of Timon's selfish quests, as the most important thing to him—surpassing all else—is loyalty to his friends. He wants to be useful, and he wants to be wanted; and what else, aside from his strength, can he offer a friend? In the end, he'll find it's quite a lot.

# SEVEN DWARFS

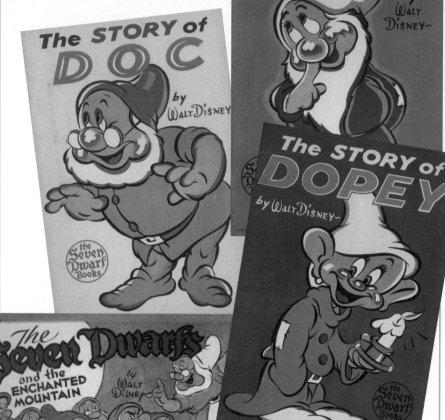

## THE FACTS

**NAME:** The Seven Dwarfs

**VOICED BY:** Pinto Colvig (Grumpy and Sleepy), Roy Atwell (Doc), Scotty Mattraw (Bashful), Billy Gilbert (Sneezy), Otis Harlan (Happy)

**DESCRIPTION:** Vertically challenged, geologically talented, poor housekeepers, generous, and loyal

## CAREER

**FILMOGRAPHY:**
*Snow White and the Seven Dwarfs*, 1937

CONFIDENTIAL

The names of the Seven Dwarfs created for Disney's film were chosen from a pool of about fifty potentials—among them, "Awful," "Hoppy," "Weepy," "Dirty," "Cranky," "Hungry," "Lazy," "Goopy," "Wistful," "Soulful," "Glick," "Crabby," "Helpful," "Tearful," "Deafy," "Thrifty," "Shifty," "Nifty," and "Burpy."

**DOC:** If the Seven Dwarfs have a leader, it has to be Doc (though he's far too good-natured to ever make it official). His mind often works faster than his mouth when he's excited, but his judgment on important decisions is usually sound.

**GRUMPY:** This know-it-all naysayer has the disposition of an old boot: tough, leathery, and resistant to anything. Like many an old boot, however, Grumpy's really a softy inside.

**BASHFUL:** More than shy, Bashful's a hopeless (make that hopeful) sentimentalist. Indeed, he can't help but blush, twist his beard, and bat his eyelashes whenever Snow White is around.

**SLEEPY:** Sleepy sneaks in his *zzz*'s anytime and anywhere he can, but nobody ever complains. Maybe that's because he works just as hard in the diamond mine as the other dwarfs, albeit in a more relaxed fashion. Even on the perpetual verge of a nap, Sleepy can be highly observant when it matters most.

**SNEEZY:** Sneezy doesn't sneeze all the time . . . just at the worst of times! He's as annoyed by his condition as the other dwarfs. But when all is said and done, his fellows are happy to lend him a sneeze-stifling hand.

**HAPPY:** Without Happy around, Grumpy might not be quite as grumpy… for Happy's just so infernally cheerful about everything!

**DOPEY:** Dubbed "Dopey" by his brothers, this loose-limbed dwarf has never spoken a word; as Happy explained to Snow White, "He never tried." But he isn't truly dopey—just childlike.

# LOST BOYS

## THE FACTS

**NAME:** The Lost Boys

**VOICED BY:** Robert Ellis, Johnny McGovern, Jeffrey Silvers, Simon "Stuffy" Singer, Tony Butala, The Mitchell Boy Choir

**DESCRIPTION:** Six wild, parentless boys for whom Never Land is a boundless playground of adventure and fun

## CAREER

**FILMOGRAPHY:**
*Peter Pan*, 1953
*Return to Never Land*, 2002

"Lost Boy" voice Stuffy Singer found his true (post-*Peter Pan*) calling in the world of sports. He was ranked nationally in table tennis, was an all-league football quarterback, won a Los Angeles tennis tournament, and became a pro baseball player at age 19! He even holds a spot in the Southern California Handball Association Hall of Fame.

"SLIGHTLY BORK" "TWINS! HEREHERE" "CURLEY HERE" "TOOTLES HERE" "HERE"

**EACH OF THE LOST BOYS WEARS A DISTINCTIVE ANIMAL COSTUME, FROM** which they derive their name and identity: Foxy, Rabbit, Skunk, the Raccoon Twins, and Cubby. They are devoted fans of Peter Pan, whom they regard as their lord and master. Although they were tempted to travel back to London with Wendy, Michael, and John and see what life was like with a "real mother," the lure of eternal youth won out in the end, and the Lost Boys remain in Never Land for everlasting adventure.

"Lost Boy" Bobby Ellis portrayed Henry Aldrich on NBC Radio's *The Aldrich Family* (1951-1953).

# FANCY FELINES

## DUCHESS AND THE KITTENS

*Berlioz is named for Hector Berlioz, the renowned French composer. Toulouse is named for the famous French artist Henri de Toulouse-Lautrec.*

**ELEGANT DUCHESS IS THE PROUD, PEDIGREED MOTHER CAT TO MARIE,** Berlioz, and Toulouse, three sweet and spoiled kitten siblings of artistic aspirations and aptitudes: Marie, who has silky white fur, a pretty pink hair ribbon, and a talent for singing; Berlioz, who is gray and favors the piano; and Toulouse, who is a redhead with a penchant for modern art. Together they live in comfort and style with the wealthy widow Madame Bonfamille. Duchess sees that her little ones are treated with the utmost care. Clever and beautiful, she possesses great strength in a crisis and excellent parenting skills.

## O'MALLEY

**O'MALLEY, A HANDSOME RED-AND-WHITE TOMCAT WITH A CHARISMATIC** smile and hipster parlance, is about as stylish as they get. A real "cool cat" with a deep-rooted wanderlust, O'Malley enjoyed walking the scene—that is, until he met Duchess and the kittens.

*O'Malley's signature song was written by the same composer who wrote "The Bare Necessities" for Baloo the bear.*

# CAPTAIN AMELIA

## THE FACTS

**NAME:** Captain Amelia

**VOICED BY:** Emma Thompson

**SIGNIFICANT OTHER:** Dr. Delbert Doppler

**DESCRIPTION:** Stoic and subtle, but acts and reacts quickly; strong, commanding, yet caring

**FAVORITE PHRASE:** "Some are big on protocol, I am big on results"

**HONORS AND AWARDS:** Amelia was awarded the Green Badge of Honor during the Kattindog Quasar War

### CAREER

**FILMOGRAPHY:** *Treasure Planet*, 2002

*While part of the Interstellar Navy, Amelia reached the rank of captain at an unusually young age. She achieved this rank by saving seven ships almost single-handedly during a space battle.*

↑ *Amelia with Doppler and Jim*

**AS THE NO-NONSENSE COMMANDER OF THE SOLAR GALLEON RLS *LEGACY*,** Amelia has a wit as lethal as her aim. Tough and clever, she's a pirate's worst nightmare, and she'll take no guff from the young pup Jim Hawkins. In the Interstellar Navy, she was a brilliant, fearless commander but was also difficult to keep under control, and grew frustrated by the bureaucracy and politics she had to deal with. Amelia has since gone on to work independently, hiring out for various endeavors.

# OLIVER

## THE FACTS

**NAME:** Oliver

**VOICED BY:** Joseph Lawrence

**DESCRIPTION:** Enthusiastic, loyal; something of a dreamer

**WORKS WELL WITH:** Jenny, Dodger, Tito (Ignacio Alonzo Julio Frederico de Tito)

**DOES NOT WORK WELL WITH:** Georgette

### CAREER

**FILMOGRAPHY:** *Oliver & Company*, 1988

← *Jenny*

**OFFICIAL** DOCUMENTS

*When Dodger sings "Why Should I Worry?" to introduce Oliver to the streets of New York, Pongo from One Hundred and One Dalmatians can be seen, as can Jock, Peg, and Trusty from Lady and the Tramp.*

**SWEET YOUNG OLIVER STARRED IN A VERSION OF DICKENS'S CLASSIC** "Oliver" story (with an animated *twist*) set in New York, with Oliver as a kitten and Fagin as the master of a pack of canine pickpockets. Oliver's personality makes an ideal bridge between kittenish cuteness and cattiness, and he is as comfortable with his ragtag existence on the streets as he is in the lap of Fifth Avenue luxury. But he is not merely a peg around which things happen; Oliver's growth as a character propels the events of the story.

# FIERCE FELINES

## THE FACTS

**NAMES:** Si and Am

**VOICED BY:** Peggy Lee

**HUMAN:** Aunt Sarah

**DESCRIPTION:** Feline grace combined with powerful destructive energy

## CAREER

**FILMOGRAPHY:**
*Lady and the Tramp,* 1955

## SI AND AM

**SI AND AM PROWL IN HARMONY, WREAKING HAVOC AS THEY GO. INNOCENT** cocker spaniel Lady often finds herself helpless to stop them from vandalizing her home, terrorizing the pet goldfish and canary, going after the baby's milk—and eventually framing her for their destructiveness.

*A 1940 script draft introduced the twin Siamese cats, then named Nip and Tuck.*

D214

## THE SIAMES

from WALT Dis

### A NOTE FROM
## FRANK AND OLLIE,
**VILLAINS DEPT.**

The Siamese cats are funny because everyone who has ever owned one has endless stories of their strange, unexpected behavior—completely self-centered (as are all cats), with aggressive personalities. There is nothing you can do with them, or about them, for that matter.

## THE FACTS

**NAME:** Lucifer

**ALSO KNOWN AS:** The household mice call him "Lucify."

**VOICED BY:** June Foray (1950); Frank Welker (2002)

**HUMAN:** Evil Lady Tremaine, always delighted to let Lucifer have his way

**DESCRIPTION:** Lazy, heavy, spoiled, and mean

## CAREER

**FILMOGRAPHY:**
*Cinderella*, 1950
*Cinderella II: Dreams Come True*, 2002

# LUCIFER

*Lucifer was modeled after animator Ward Kimball's own cat. Once Walt Disney saw Kimball's furry calico, he declared, "There's your Lucifer."*

### A WORD FROM
# WARD

Walt always thought cats were villains.

**LUCIFER IS A BIG, FAT, USELESS CAT THAT TAKES ADVANTAGE OF EVERY** chance to make the whole world accommodate his desires. Lethargic, indolent, and a ruthless bully, he's an extra threat because he is also quick, strong, and clever.

## THE FACTS

**NAME:** Cheshire Cat

**VOICED BY:** Sterling Holloway

**DESCRIPTION:** Confusing, comic, and mad

**SPECIAL NOTE:** Keep tooth-whitener on hand

## CAREER

**FILMOGRAPHY:**
*Alice in Wonderland*, 1951

*Lewis Carroll, author of <u>Alice's Adventures in Wonderland</u>, was a native of Cheshire, England.*

# CHESHIRE CAT

*Traditionally, Cheshire cheeses were molded into the shape of a smiling cat and eaten from the tail, leaving only the grinning head on the plate.*

**BEARING PINK AND PURPLE STRIPES AND SINGING OF THE JABBERWOCK,** the Cheshire Cat has a tendency to appear at critical moments, and disappear just as inconveniently. With his strange dialogue and dreamy grin, he's been known to engage Alice in amusing but quite vexing conversation, and he often points out thoughts and ideas that annoy her.

# COOL CANINES

## LADY

### THE FACTS

**NAME:** Lady

**NICKNAME:** Pidge

**VOICED BY:** Barbara Luddy (1955); Jodi Benson (2001)

**SIGNIFICANT OTHER:** Tramp

**HUMANS:** Jim Dear and Darling

**BREED:** Cocker spaniel

**DESCRIPTION:** Loyal and loving

**SPECIAL NOTE:** Loves pasta!

### CAREER

**FILMOGRAPHY:**
*Lady and the Tramp*, 1955
*Lady and the Tramp II: Scamp's Adventure*, 2001

**RAISED IN DOMESTIC SAFETY AND COMFORT,** Lady is thoroughly faithful to her adoring humans, and knows little of the hostile world a dog can face beyond the privilege of the "collar-and-leash set." Despite her best efforts, she found herself falling head over paws for a handsome charmer named Tramp—a dog from the wrong side of the tracks who set about showing her that while there's danger in the "outside world," there's also life.

## TRAMP

STUDIO CIRCULATION ONLY

### THE FACTS

**NAME:** Tramp

**VOICED BY:** Larry Roberts (1955); Jeff Bennett (2001)

**SIGNIFICANT OTHER:** Lady

**BREED:** Mutt

**DESCRIPTION:** Cocky, carefree, and confident

**WORKS WELL WITH:** Just about anyone sensitive to his canine charms

### CAREER

**FILMOGRAPHY:**
*Lady and the Tramp*, 1955
*Lady and the Tramp II: Scamp's Adventure*, 2001

**FOOTLOOSE AND COLLAR-FREE, TRAMP** lived every day as if it were his last. Although he was always just one step ahead of the dogcatcher, Tramp was too busy playing with danger to be scared of it. He's that rare breed of dog that wants no master but himself. Living by his wits, he learned that if you have a little charm and a lot of finesse, the world can be your dinner bowl. He was an irresistible rogue with a weakness for the ladies…until he met Lady.

...and *NOW* his **Happiest** Motion Picture!

**Walt Disney's** *Lady* AND THE *Tramp*

*In early scripts, Tramp was first called "Homer," then "Rags," and even "Bozo."*

## THE FACTS

**NAME:** Heather Lad o' Glencairn

**NICKNAME:** Jock

**VOICED BY:** Bill Thompson

**BREED:** Scottish terrier

**DESCRIPTION:** Plucky and smart, tiny but tough

## CAREER

**FILMOGRAPHY:**
*Lady and the Tramp*, 1955
*Lady and the Tramp II:
Scamp's Adventure*, 2001

# JOCK

**JOCK IS THE EPITOME OF THE SCOTTISH TERRIER, FROM HIS STUBBY** physique to his slightly gruff personality tempered by his good nature. His sensitivity and caring are apparent in the way he protects his friend Trusty from the truth about his lost sense of smell, and his keening reaction to Trusty's brave collision with the dog-pound wagon. Although protective of Lady and suspicious of Tramp, Jock always does his best to protect the mutt.

## THE FACTS

**NAME:** Trusty

**VOICED BY:** Bill Baucom

**CLOSE RELATIVES:** Old Reliable (Grandpappy)

**BREED:** Bloodhound

**DESCRIPTION:** Generally doleful, but genial and faithful

**NOTE:** Rests a lot

## CAREER

**FILMOGRAPHY:**
*Lady and the Tramp*, 1955
*Lady and the Tramp II:
Scamp's Adventure*, 2001

# TRUSTY

**A BLOODHOUND OF DISTINGUISHED LINEAGE, POOR TRUSTY HAS** completely lost his sense of smell, a fact well known to all of his friends, who dutifully protect this secret. He is built like a standard bloodhound: fifteen pounds of dog in a wrinkly twenty-pound bag. His Southern drawl and moonlight-and-magnolias chivalry make him a great protector of Lady, and even Tramp, for whom he loyally (almost) lays down his life.

# SPOTTED SPECIMENS

## PONGO

### THE FACTS

**NAME:** Pongo

**VOICED BY:** Rod Taylor (1961); Samuel West (2003)

**SIGNIFICANT OTHER:** Perdita

**CLOSE RELATIVES:** Ninety-nine puppies (natural dad of fifteen)

**HUMAN:** Roger Radcliff

**BREED:** Dalmatian

**DESCRIPTION:** Urbane, sophisticated, and handsome

**SPECIAL SKILLS:** The Twilight Bark

### CAREER

**FILMOGRAPHY:** [see *Perdita*]

**PONGO WAS LONDON'S MOST ELIGIBLE CANINE—A SINGLE DOG LIVING** the bachelor life with his "pet human," songwriter Roger—until he spotted the lovely Perdita "walking" her human Anita. The dapper Dalmatian immediately took matters into his own paws and arranged an introduction. (How could Perdita resist?) Marriage, a new home…and a bouncing family of puppies soon followed, making Pongo a proud and loving father (and the best dog in the world, as far as the pups are concerned) who won't let anything stand in the way of his family's safety— not even the peculiar interests of that bizarre woman, Cruella De Vil.

## PERDITA

### THE FACTS

**NAME:** Perdita

**VOICED BY:** Cate Bauer (1961); Kath Soucie (2003)

**SIGNIFICANT OTHER:** Pongo

**CLOSE RELATIVES:** Ninety-nine puppies (natural mom of fifteen)

**HUMAN:** Anita

**DESCRIPTION:** Quiet and refined, poised and lovely

### CAREER

**FILMOGRAPHY:**
*One Hundred and One Dalmatians*, 1961
*101 Dalmatians*, 1997 (TV series)
*Mickey's House of Villains*, 2002
*101 Dalmatians II: Patch's London Adventure*, 2003

**PERDITA WASN'T TOO SURE ABOUT THE RAFFISH PONGO ON FIRST** meeting, but she has never regretted their union. When she and her mate were blessed with a healthy and rambunctious litter of pups, she would've been the happiest dog around—if it weren't for her uneasy premonitions about that "devil" Cruella. Perdita's a dog that trusts her intuition. So when her babies vanished, she knew exactly who took them. And while she loves the comforts of hearth and home, she's willing to leave them behind and take on any frightening journey necessary to save her beloved children—as long as her dashing mate is by her side.

## THE FACTS

**NAMES:** *No room here! See attached list.*

**VOICED BY:** Barbara Beaird (Rolly), Micky Maga (Patch), Sandra Abbott (Penny), Mimi Gibson (Lucky)

## CAREER

**FILMOGRAPHY:**
*One Hundred and One Dalmatians,* 1961
*101 Dalmatians,* 1997 (TV series)
*Mickey's House of Villains,* 2002
*101 Dalmatians II: Patch's London Adventure,* 2003

# NINETY-NINE DALMATIAN PUPPIES

*Tips for telling them apart:*

- The boy pups wear red collars (like Pongo)
- The girl pups wear blue collars (like Perdita)
- Patch has a black patch around his eye
- Lucky has two black ears and a horseshoe-shaped pattern on his back
- Rolly's a bit pudgier than the others
- Freckles has a few spots on his nose
- Penny has the fewest spots of all
- (You're on your own for the rest)

**THESE PUPS MAY BE DIFFICULT TO TELL APART, BUT FROM THE MOMENT** the first fifteen of them arrived during a dark and stormy night, their individual personalities were set. Lucky, the runt of the litter, likes television—maybe a little too much. Rolly's always ready for a snack. Patch talks a big game; if he had to face TV bad-guy Dirty Dawson, he sure wouldn't let that "yellow-livered old varmint" escape. Still, the pups do have one important thing in common, and that's a dose of bravery much bigger than they are. When Cruella De Vil puppy-napped them away from hearth and home, these kids chipped right in to save their own spotted skins.

# DOG (AND FOX) POUND

## THE FACTS

**NAMES:** Copper and Tod

**VOICED BY:** Corey Feldman, Kurt Russell (Copper); Keith Coogan, Mickey Rooney (Tod)

**BREED:** Bloodhound (Copper)

**DESCRIPTION:** Copper's a loud, clumsy, happy hound dog; Tod's a sharp, fun-loving, fast fox

## CAREER

**FILMOGRAPHY:**
*The Fox and the Hound*, 1981

## TOD AND COPPER

*The Fox and the Hound* remains unusual among Disney films in that it does not have a traditional happy ending.

↖ *Young Copper with Slade's older dog, Chief.*

**ORPHANED AS A YOUNG FOX KIT,** Tod was taken under the wing of a kindly owl named Big Mama, who arranged for him to be adopted by the compassionate Widow Tweed on her farm. Shortly after, Tweed's neighbor, the ill-tempered hunter Amos Slade, brought home a young hound pup named Copper. The two young animals met and quickly formed an unlikely friendship—one they knew would last forever.

## THE FACTS

**NAME:** Doctor Delbert Doppler

**VOICED BY:** David Hyde Pierce

**SIGNIFICANT OTHER:** Captain Amelia

**BREED:** Good question

**DESCRIPTION:** Intelligent, erudite, shy, awkward, wealthy

**SPECIAL SKILLS:** Speaks fluent Flatula

## CAREER

**FILMOGRAPHY:** *Treasure Planet*, 2002

STUDIO CIRCULATION ONLY

# DOCTOR DOPPLER

**A BOOKISH BACHELOR WITH A YEN FOR ADVENTURE, THE DOGLIKE** Doppler is somewhat lacking in social skills, but makes up for it with his brave heart and courageous spirit. He's a butterfly ready to emerge from his nerdy cocoon.

Charged by Jim's mother with chaperoning her errant son during the journey to Treasure Planet, Doppler quickly found himself an egghead out of water amongst the motley crew of hardened space sailors. But when a mutiny erupted, Doppler displayed real courage under fire—and snared the heart of a certain finicky feline.

## THE FACTS

**NAME:** Dodger

**VOICED BY:** Billy Joel

**BREED:** Mutt

**DESCRIPTION:** Street-smart brown-spotted mongrel

**SKILLS:** Singing, pickpocketing

**FAVORITE PHRASE:** "Absitively posolutely!"

## CAREER

**FILMOGRAPHY:** *Oliver & Company*, 1988

# DODGER

**COCKY DODGER—NEW YORK'S SELF-TITLED "COOLEST QUADRUPED"—** first came across a little orange cat lost in the streets and recruited him to steal sausages from a hot dog vendor. After running back to share the booty with his canine pals—Tito, Einstein, Rita, and Francis—Dodger discovered that the cat had followed him home...and was about to launch them all into a big adventure.

# TIMOTHY Q. MOUSE

## THE FACTS

**NAME:** Timothy Q. Mouse

**VOICED BY:** Edward Brophy

**DESCRIPTION:** Feisty, tough, and protective, with a strength and personality far bigger than his half-pint size

**DOES NOT WORK WELL WITH:** Gossipy elephants, mean clowns, cruel crows, champagne

**SPECIAL NOTE:** Doesn't mind when a job pays peanuts

## CAREER

**FILMOGRAPHY:**
*Dumbo,* 1941

*Tipsy, but still on the ball*

*While trying to comfort Dumbo, Timothy says, "Lots of people with big ears are famous!" That's a joke on Walt Disney himself, who did, in fact, have big ears.*

**STUDIO CIRCULATION ONLY**

**TIMOTHY IS A PRETTY CONVENTIONAL-LOOKING LITTLE BROWN MOUSE—** except for his very dapper circus ringmaster uniform and his high-volume, Brooklyn-accented pipes. He is not only protective of baby Jumbo, he has a faith in the little fellow that no one but Mrs. Jumbo shares. "What's the matter wid his ears?" Timothy asks. "I don't see nothin' wrong with 'em. I tink they're cute!"

2006 9 5

2006 9 5

WALT DISNEY'S

# DUMBO

ONLY HIS
EARS GREW!

One of Timothy's most
memorable and endearing traits
is his distinctive voice, provided
by Edward Brophy, in his first
and last cartoon role.

# GUS AND JAQ

## THE FACTS

**NAMES:** Gus and Jaq

**ALSO KNOWN AS:** Octavius or Gus-Gus (Gus) and Jacques (Jaq)

**VOICED BY:**
Jimmy Macdonald (1950);
Corey Burton (2002)

**SIGNIFICANT OTHER:** They have eyes for no one except their generous protector and benefactress, Cinderella

**CLOSE RELATIVES:** Luke (the smallest), Mert and Bert (the twins), Suzy, Perla, and Blossom

**DESCRIPTION:** Loyal, protective, helpful, happy, and hungry (well, Gus, at least)

**DO NOT WORK WELL WITH:** Cats, large keys in combination with steep staircases

## CAREER

**FILMOGRAPHY:**
Cinderella, 1950
Cinderella II: Dreams
  Come True, 2002

During their comic book career, the two little mice moved from the Tremaine château into the castle, along with their friend Cinderella. Their rival, Lucifer, tried to follow them and continue his torments, but by royal decree, cats were banned from within the castle walls (Walt Disney's Christmas Parade #2, 1950).

Disney story man Winston Hibler termed the high-pitched, speedy, almost-unintelligible language of Gus, Jaq, and their friends "Mouse Latin."

**JAQ IS SKINNY, WIRY, AND QUICK—BOTH ON HIS FEET AND WITH HIS** wits—and he's got streetwise smarts around the house and its obstacles.

Gus is chubby, tubby, lovable, and a bit slow—both on his feet and with his wits. He counts on the support and help of his friends, but shows great courage and strength when confronted with real danger.

Gus and Jaq make one of many print appearances in 1950.

Luke →

← Suzy

gus →

← Jaq

← Little mice,
big energy

**FROM THE DESK OF**

## WALT DISNEY

To some [timeless] stories, a film
version can give wider scope
and even add characters without
damage to the original tale.
In *Cinderella*... there was every
proof that audiences enjoyed
our addition of the mice
characters, Gus and Jaq, and the
valiant, fun-loving little
band of Cinderella's helpers.

**OTHER MICE:** Gus and Jaq

# BERNARD AND BIANCA

## THE FACTS

**NAMES:** Bernard and Bianca

**ALSO KNOWN AS:** The Rescuers

**VOICED BY:**
Bob Newhart (Bernard),
Eva Gabor (Bianca)

**SIGNIFICANT OTHERS:** One another, sweetly and shyly

**DESCRIPTION:** Little white mice with big hearts and king-sized courage

**BERNARD DOES NOT WORK WELL WITH:** Alligators, pipe organs, lizards, air travel in general, the number thirteen

## CAREER

**FILMOGRAPHY:**
*The Rescuers*, 1977
*The Rescuers Down Under*, 1990

*The Rescuers films were inspired by the novels The Rescuers and Miss Bianca by Margery Sharp.*

with Penny →

**BIANCA IS A STYLISH, SOPHISTICATED, CONFIDENT, AND ADVENTUROUS** Hungarian mouse who is respected within the ranks of the Rescue Aid Society (a worldwide mouse assistance organization) for all of these attributes.

Bernard is a shy, tongue-tied, modest mouse who works as the janitor at the RAS Headquarters in New York. Bernard is also superstitious, suffers from Triskaidekaphobia (irrational fear of the number thirteen), and hates flying. But when the situation demands it, he is resourceful and courageous.

## CASE HISTORIES:

• The Rescue Aid Society found a plea for help from a little orphan girl named Penny, whereupon Bianca and Bernard took up the case, and—after avoiding two brutish crocodiles, enlisting the help of the local swamp folk, and turning the villain Medusa and her henchmen against each other—ultimately came to Penny's rescue.

• In Australia, a young boy named Cody discovered that a poacher had captured the magnificent eagle Marahute. He managed to set her free only to be kidnapped himself and later to see her recaptured. A frantic call went out to the Rescue Aid Society, which brought the intrepid Bernard and Miss Bianca rushing to Cody's aid.

When Eva Gabor was cast as Miss Bianca, the character was given Eva's Hungarian nationality, making Miss Bianca Hungary's representative to the Rescue Aid Society.

Joanna sees Bernard as potential supper.

## THE FACTS

**NAME:** Basil

**ALSO KNOWN AS:** Basil of Baker Street

**VOICED BY:** Barrie Ingham

**DESCRIPTION:** Brilliant, baffling, moody, intense

**FAVORITE PHRASE:** "The game is afoot!"

**SPECIAL SKILLS:** Deductive reasoning, crime-scene analysis

## CAREER

**FILMOGRAPHY:**
*The Great Mouse Detective*, 1986

# BASIL

*The Great Mouse Detective is based on the book Basil of Baker Street by author Eve Titus.*

**THE WORLD'S GREATEST MOUSE DETECTIVE HAS A MIND THAT CAN SWING** from the height of triumph to the depths of despair in the blink of an eye: triumph, when he thinks he's close to catching his evil nemesis, Ratigan; despair, when the cad slips through his fingers once again. For comfort, he turns to his trusty violin. Basil has amazing powers of deduction ("Offhand, I can deduce only little, only that the list is written with a broad-pointed pen . . . the paper is of native Mongolian manufacture . . . and has been gummed, unless I'm very much mistaken, by a bat that has been drinking Rodent's Delight!") and uses them to help his clients in trouble. His goal is to get Professor Ratigan behind bars and rescue Olivia Flaversham's father—while saving the monarchy, to boot.

## THE FACTS

**NAME:** Dr. David Q. Dawson

**VOICED BY:** Val Bettin

**DESCRIPTION:** Bumfuzzled, loyal, protective, and unwittingly courageous

## CAREER

**FILMOGRAPHY:**
*The Great Mouse Detective*, 1986

# DR. DAWSON

*A series of comics based on Basil and Dawson were released, but they were available only in Finland, Sweden, and Germany.*

*Masters of disguise*

**DAWSON IS SOMETHING OF A CHUBBY BUMBLER, WHO IS REDEEMED BY** his good heart. Previously of the Queen's 66th Regiment in Afghanistan, Dawson is constantly amazed by Basil's powers of deduction. The mouse met Basil after bringing Olivia Flaversham to Baker Street, and eventually became Basil's associate, friend, and personal biographer.

## THE FACTS

**NAMES:** Hiram and Olivia Flaversham

**DESCRIPTION:** Short and sweet

**VOICED BY:** Susanne Pollatschek (Olivia), Alan Young (Hiram)

## CAREER

**FILMOGRAPHY:**
*The Great Mouse Detective*, 1986

# HIRAM AND OLIVIA

**OLIVIA FLAVERSHAM IS A TINY SLIP OF A GIRL OF SCOTTISH DESCENT,** who sought Basil's help in finding her toymaker father, Hiram. When Olivia and Dr. Dawson arrived on his doorstep, the great mouse detective couldn't be bothered—until he deduced that the seemingly simple Case of the Missing Toymaker might actually involve a fiendish plot that could lead straight to his nemesis, Professor Ratigan!

## THE FACTS

**NAME:** Roquefort

**VOICED BY:** Sterling Holloway

**DESCRIPTION:** Brave, clever, and loyal; a quick-witted detective

**NOTABLE QUOTE:** "Please! I was sent for help by a cat!"

## CAREER

**FILMOGRAPHY:**
*The Aristocats*, 1970

*Sterling Holloway's first voice for Walt Disney was that of Mr. Stork in Dumbo. He was also the adult Flower in Bambi, Kaa in The Jungle Book, and the Cheshire Cat in Alice in Wonderland.*

# ROQUEFORT

THIS MATERIAL
PROPERTY
THE WALT DISNEY
IT I JNPUBLISHE

*Roquefort is a ewe's-milk blue cheese from the south of France. Though similar cheeses are produced elsewhere, French law dictates that only those cheeses aged in the caves of Roquefort-sur-Soulzon may bear the name "Roquefort."*

**ROQUEFORT LIVES IN THE MANSION OF MADAME BONFAMILLE, AND IS** a good friend to the "Aristocats": Duchess, Marie, Berlioz, and Toulouse.

When Roquefort learned that the cats had gone missing, he donned his Inverness cape and deerstalker cap, and set out to look for them. In the end, little Roquefort put his own life at risk by entering a "lion's den" of hostile cats in order to help rescue his feline friends.

## THE FACTS

**NAME:** Bambi

**VOICED BY:** Bobby Stewart; Donnie Dunagan; Hardie Albright; John Sutherland

**SIGNIFICANT OTHER:** Faline

**MOTHER:** "Mother"

**FATHER:** The Great Prince of the Forest

**DESCRIPTION:** Innocent, childlike

**SPECIAL SKILLS:** Ice skating

## CAREER

**FILMOGRAPHY:**
*Bambi*, 1942
*Bambi II*, 2006

*Bambi* is based on a book published in 1928 by the Viennese author Felix Salten.

**BAMBI IS THE WOBBLY-LEGGED FAWN WITH A FUTURE IN STORE AS "GREAT** Prince of the Forest." For now, though, he has his mother to teach him the secrets of survival, and his pals, Thumper and Flower, to help him explore the secret of fun. Too soon, Man's arrival in the forest will bring Bambi's carefree days to a tragic end. If he's to endure the harsh winter, he'll have to learn how to stand alone. Even then, it will only be his first life challenge, as the coming spring heralds the new dangers of finding and protecting a mate. More than Bambi's life, the very survival of the forest could hang in the balance of the young prince's courage.

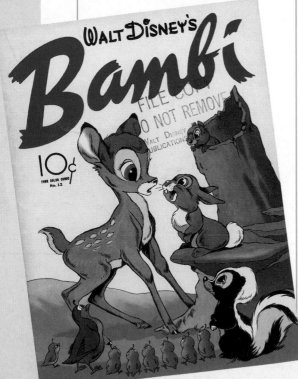

# THUMPER AND FLOWER

## THE FACTS

**NAME:** Thumper

**VOICED BY:** Peter Behn; Sam Edwards

**DESCRIPTION:** Energetic, gregarious, athletic, plucky, and candid

**NOTABLE QUOTE:** "If you can't say something nice...don't say nothin' at all."

## CAREER

**FILMOGRAPHY:**
Bambi, 1942
Bambi II, 2006

### THUMPER

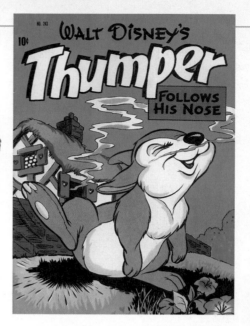

*Human models were used for one scene: actress Jane Randolph and Ice Capades star Donna Atwood acted as live-action references for Bambi and Thumper's misadventure on ice.*

**THUMPER IS BAMBI'S FIRST FOREST PAL,** a vigorous boy bunny who finds excitement in every discovery of the world around him. He encourages Bambi in endeavors ranging from his first steps to ice skating to his first kiss.

## THE FACTS

**NAME:** Flower

**VOICED BY:** Stan Alexander; Sterling Holloway

**DESCRIPTION:** Painfully shy, sweet-natured, friendly

**NOTABLE QUOTE:** "He can call me 'Flower,' if he wants to..."

## CAREER

**FILMOGRAPHY:**
Bambi, 1942
Bambi II, 2006

### FLOWER

**AN ELEGANT BLACK-AND-WHITE** boy skunk whose bashful nature is belied by his natural scent. No matter his fragrance, he's always a Flower, and always a loyal friend to Bambi and Thumper.

**FROM THE DESK OF**

**WALT DISNEY**

Those personalities are just pure gold.

# BRER BEASTIES

## THE FACTS

**NAME:** Brer Rabbit

**VOICED BY:** Johnny Lee

**DESCRIPTION:** Quick, clever, cocky, smart, and sassy

## CAREER

**FILMOGRAPHY:**
*Song of the South,* 1946

### BRER RABBIT

**BRER RABBIT IS THE MOST OUT-DOIN'-EST, BODACIOUS CRITTER IN THE** whole world. Being little, and without much strength, he's supposed to use his head instead of his feet, and that's what he does. Every time he gets in a fix with Brer Fox and Brer Bear, he gets himself out of trouble by using his wits. Some escapes are easier than others, but in the end, Brer Rabbit always comes out on top.

*When the recording session for the "Laughing Place" sequence was scheduled, Johnny Lee was away on a USO tour. James Baskett filled in, recording both Brer Fox's and Brer Rabbit's dialog.*

## THE FACTS

**NAME:** Brer Fox

**VOICED BY:** James Baskett

**DESCRIPTION:**

*James Baskett spoke the part of Brer Fox so quickly that the animators were unable to sync their animation with complete accuracy. Animators Frank Thomas and Ollie Johnston calculated that Baskett spoke about eight words a second, or one-eighth of a second per word!*

# BRER FOX

**BRER FOX IS A SLY AND SMART** backwoods red fox, regularly cooking up schemes to catch that pesky Brer Rabbit. The rabbit's cockiness usually brings him awfully close to Brer Fox's stew pot—and oh, does Brer Fox crave fresh rabbit stew! If it weren't for Brer Bear, he might have had it by now!

MATERIAL IS THE
PPERTY OF
DISNEY COMPANY.
PUBLISHED AND
BE TAKEN

## THE FACTS

**NAME:** Brer Bear

**VOICED BY:** Nicodemus Stewart

**DESCRIPTION:** Big, brawny, and boneheaded

**FAVORITE PHRASE:** "I'm gonna knock his head clean off!"

## CAREER

**FILMOGRAPHY:** *Song of the South*, 1946

# BRER BEAR

*At the age of 79, Nicodemus Stewart was a guest of honor at the opening of Splash Mountain at Disneyland, a ride featuring the Song of the South critters.*

**BRER BEAR IS BIG ON BRAWN, BUT SMALL ON BRAINS. HE'S ALWAYS** ready to make his point with a club—thinking things through isn't this bear's strength. Although frequently his bumbling gets between Brer Fox and his rabbit stew, the fox is smart enough to know that Brer Bear makes a better sidekick than adversary.

# FOREST FAUNA ▶ RABBITS

## THE FACTS

**NAME:** White Rabbit

**VOICED BY:** Bill Thompson

**SPECIAL NOTE:** Usually tardy to the set

## CAREER

**FILMOGRAPHY:**
*Alice in Wonderland*, 1951

*Fastidious to a fault, but an organizational whiz!*

## WHITE RABBIT

*Morpheus's instruction to Neo to "follow the white rabbit" in the science fiction film <u>The Matrix</u> has its source in this character.*

**THE WHITE RABBIT HAS SEVERE ANXIETY ISSUES ABOUT PROMPTNESS,** which he persistently announces to the world at large. He is capable of fretting about many other things, too. (This curious creature is the reason Alice fell down the rabbit hole and ended up in Wonderland.)

*"White Rabbit" is the title of one of the most popular songs by the rock group Jefferson Airplane. The song includes several other references to characters in Lewis Carroll's tale.*

## THE FACTS

**NAME:** March Hare

**VOICED BY:** Jerry Colonna

**NOTABLE QUOTE:**
"I have an excellent idea—
let's change the subject!"

## CAREER

**FILMOGRAPHY:**
*Alice in Wonderland*, 1951

# MARCH HARE

*"Mad as a march hare" was a common phrase in author Lewis Carroll's time. The saying refers to the hare's madcap behavior at the beginning of the long breeding season, which lasts from February to September.*

**LONG-EARED, WILD-EYED, AND BUCK-TOOTHED, ON COMPARISON IT IS** difficult to decide whether the Hare or the Hatter is most mad. The Hare finds his mallet handy for delicate business such as watch repair, and he quite enjoys a good cup of tea.

# MAD HATTER

STUDIO CIRCULATION ONLY

**VOICED BY:** Ed Wynn

**THE HATTER IS NATURALLY QUITE MAD,** and speaks with a dopey voice and pronounced lisp. His solution to most questions is simply to further muddle the issue. Together with the Hare and the dozy little Dormouse, he created a maddening afternoon for Alice.

*Note: Constantly breaks for tea-time.*

# FOREST FAUNA ▶ KENAI

## THE FACTS

**NAME:** Kenai

**VOICED BY:** Joaquin Phoenix

**RELATIVES:** Denahi, Sitka (brothers)

**DESCRIPTION:** Teenaged and troubled; angry, confused—and lost

## CAREER

**FILMOGRAPHY:**
Brother Bear, 2003

**YOUNG KENAI TENDS TO RACE THROUGH LIFE IN HIGH GEAR, ANXIOUS** to prove himself as a man to his two older brothers.

When he was magically transformed into a bear by the Great Spirits, he began a life-altering journey to where the lights touch the earth, hoping to regain his human form—learning a valuable life lesson about love and brotherhood.

Kenai, in human form, with his older brothers, Denahi and Sitka.
↓

Originally, Kenai was supposed to have an older bear named Grizz guide him through the woods and become like a brother to him. Grizz was eventually replaced by Koda, although it's not erroneous to think that Tug bears an uncanny similarity to Grizz.

# FOREST FAUNA ▶ KODA

## THE FACTS

**NAME:** Koda

**VOICED BY:** Jeremy Suarez

**DESCRIPTION:** Youthful, vigorous, garrulous, and cheerful

## CAREER

**FILMOGRAPHY:**
*Brother Bear*, 2003

In the vignettes during the end credits of *Brother Bear*, Kenai is shown drawing a crude stick figure on a rock, while Koda finishes an Impressionist painting that suspiciously resembles *A Sunday Afternoon on the Island of La Grande Jatte* by Georges Seurat.

## DESCRIPTION

CONFIDENT[...]

**KODA IS AN IRREPRESSIBLE BEAR CUB, A STRAIGHT-**arrow, true-blue youth who's very confident in himself and secure in his views. He jabbers a mile a minute and never sits still. Gregarious and enthusiastic, Koda always has a story to tell and a new friend to make.

While on a mission to join his mother at the annual bear family reunion at the Salmon Run, he found a traveling companion in Kenai, and their two journeys became one. As they traveled together, Koda became Kenai's guide and companion, helping him discover what the natural world is all about.

## THE FACTS

**NAME:** Dumbo

**ALSO KNOWN AS:** Baby Jumbo

**MOTHER:** Mrs. Jumbo

**MENTOR:** Timothy Q. Mouse

**DESCRIPTION:** Small, cute, and sweet as can be

**DOES NOT WORK WELL WITH:** Clowns; mean, gossipy, or pink elephants

## CAREER

**FILMOGRAPHY:**
*Dumbo*, 1941

**HONORS AND AWARDS:**
1942 Academy Award for Best Music, Scoring of a Musical Picture: Frank Churchill, Oliver Wallace

1942 Academy Award nominee for Best Original Song: "Baby Mine" Frank Churchill (music), Ned Washington (lyrics)

1947 Cannes Film Festival Award for Best Animation Design (*Prix du meilleur dessin animé*)

*Mrs. Jumbo (Dumbo's mother) only speaks once, when she says Dumbo's real name.*

**TAUNTED FOR THE SIZE OF HIS ENORMOUS EARS, THE LITTLE ELEPHANT** Dumbo was too young to understand what the laughter was about but old enough to know that it was aimed at him. Cruelly separated from his mother by the circus and misunderstood and mistreated by the other animals, he was all alone in the world with "no warm trunk to cuddle up to, no one to dry his tears." Fortunately, he had a mouse in his corner—Timothy Q. Mouse. With his new friend's help and guidance (and the help of a "magic feather"), Dumbo found the courage to take the leap of faith that turned the taunting into cheers, and made all his dreams soar.

*Dumbo is the only Disney animated feature film with a title character that doesn't speak.*

*Legend has it that Dumbo was scheduled for the cover of the December 29, 1941 issue of Time magazine. The onset of the war established different priorities, and instead of the genial baby elephant, the stern visage of General Douglas MacArthur glowered from the newsstands.*

# ORVILLE AND WILBUR

## THE FACTS

**NAME:** Orville Albatross

**VOICED BY:** Jim Jordan

**SIBLING:** Wilbur Albatross

**DESCRIPTION:** Confident, cranky—and just a bit clumsy

**NOTABLE QUOTE:** "Any landing is a good one as long as you can walk away from it."

## CAREER

**FILMOGRAPHY:**
*The Rescuers*, 1977

*Orville was animated by Ollie Johnston, with an able assist from Chuck Harvey.*

## THE FACTS

**NAME:** Wilbur Albatross

**VOICED BY:** John Candy

**SIBLING:** Orville Albatross

**DESCRIPTION:** Ebullient, loud—and just a bit gauche

**BUSINESS SLOGAN:** "Albatross Air, a fair fare from here to there."

## CAREER

**FILMOGRAPHY:**
*The Rescuers Down Under*, 1990

## ORVILLE

*Jim Jordan, the voice of Orville Albatross, was the star of the Fibber McGee and Molly radio program from 1935 until 1959. For many years it was the top-rated radio program in America.*

**A MIXTURE OF CRISP YOUTH AND GENIAL OLDSTER, ORVILLE IS A PEAR-**shaped, aviator cap–wearing seabird and the proprietor of the New York–based Albatross Air Charter Service. Happy to be of service wherever his flight skills allow, Orville helped intrepid mice Bernard and Bianca rescue Penny from Madame Medusa's evil designs.

## WILBUR

**NATURALLY SIMILAR IN APPEARANCE TO SIBLING ORVILLE ALBATROSS,** Wilbur is a big buffoon with a heart of gold—with approximately the same grace at aviation as his brother. He proved instrumental in transporting Bernard and Bianca on their whirlwind journey to save young Cody and golden eagle Marahute from the murderous Percival McLeach.

## THE HUMAN TOUCH ▶ ESMERALDA

### THE FACTS

**NAME:** Esmeralda

**VOICED BY:** Demi Moore (speaking), Heidi Mollenhauer (singing)

**SIGNIFICANT OTHERS:** Phoebus, Quasimodo

**PET:** Djali (a talented goat)

**DESCRIPTION:** Free, fearless, somewhat mysterious, exotic, graceful

### CAREER

**FILMOGRAPHY:**
*The Hunchback of Notre Dame*, 1996
*The Hunchback of Notre Dame II*, 2002

A4-16A

A4-20

**ESMERALDA IS A BIT DIFFERENT FROM** other heroines. She's physically stronger and tougher, yet because she herself is an outcast and has been discriminated against, she has the capacity to sympathize and relate to Quasimodo as no one has before. Esmeralda lives the life of a Gypsy, and when she dances the coins of admirers fall at her feet—and the hearts of men are filled with desire. When one day she danced into danger, only the walls of Notre Dame could save her from certain death.

# THE HUMAN TOUCH ▶ PHOEBUS

## THE FACTS

**NAME:** Phoebus

**VOICED BY:** Kevin Kline

**SIGNIFICANT OTHER:** Esmeralda

**HORSE:** Achilles (a stalwart stallion)

**DESCRIPTION:** Brave, handsome, but with a wry sense of humor

## CAREER

**FILMOGRAPHY:**
*The Hunchback of Notre Dame*, 1996
*The Hunchback of Notre Dame II*, 2002

A4-17A

**PHOEBUS, THE CAPTAIN OF THE GUARD, IS MORE SYMPATHETIC AND** humane than his comrades in arms, but just as susceptible to the beguiling charms of the hypnotic Esmeralda. One day as he was thundering down the cobblestones astride his horse, Achilles, he tossed a gold coin into a beggar's hat—except that when he looked a second time, he discovered the beggar was actually a certain beautiful Gypsy in disguise.

While Phoebus's personality contains elements of courage, humor, and sensibility, on the whole he's still something of a cipher.

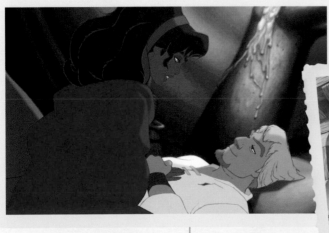

# THE HUMAN TOUCH ▶ TARZAN

*Although in this film Clayton is the villain, in the book series, it is Tarzan's birth name: John Clayton, Earl of Greystoke.*

## THE FACTS

**NAME:** Tarzan

**VOICED BY:** Tony Goldwyn

**SIGNIFICANT OTHER:** Jane Porter

**FOSTER FATHER:** Kerchak

**FOSTER MOTHER:** Kala

**SIDEKICKS:** Terk (gregarious girl gorilla) and Tantor (overly anxious elephant)

**DESCRIPTION:** Lean, muscled, graceful, and athletic; also clever and kindly—yet confused about who he is and his place in the world

## CAREER

**FILMOGRAPHY:**
Tarzan, 1999
Tarzan & Jane, 2002
Tarzan, 2003
   (TV series)
Tarzan II, 2005
"Tarzan," 2006
   (Theatrical show)

"Tarzan is a great role because the range of this character is enormous. He can be comical and silly and childlike and yet there's a whole drama to the story that is very serious, intense, and emotional."

—TONY GOLDWYN

**ORPHANED AS AN INFANT, RAISED BY A FAMILY OF GORILLAS, AND** ultimately accepted as one of their own, Tarzan is a young man with all the instincts of a jungle animal and the physical prowess of an athletic superstar. He is at one with the animals—speaking with them, living with them, learning from them. His life was forever changed when he finally met other humans—with whom he felt an immediate and irresistible bond.

*Several treatments were written for a Disney Tarzan animated feature way back in the 1930s, but the project never came to fruition.*

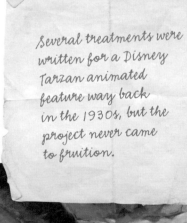

## THE FACTS

**NAME:** Jane Porter

**VOICED BY:** Minnie Driver

**SIGNIFICANT OTHER:** Tarzan ("A man with no language, no human behavior. And no respect for personal boundaries.")

**FATHER:** Professor Porter

**MOTHER:** Deceased

**DESCRIPTION:** Pretty and perky, with a no-nonsense, intellectual sense of purpose and a respect for nature

## CAREER

**FILMOGRAPHY:**
Tarzan, 1999
Tarzan & Jane, 2002
Tarzan, 2003
   (TV series)
Tarzan II, 2005
"Tarzan," 2006
   (Theatrical show)

"I knew how I wanted Jane to be from the start. She was never going to be a boring Victorian heroine. She had to be something original.... She's very adventurous, funny, and gutsy.... She's completely non-judgmental about the world around her. She's curious and very resourceful. She's also extremely devoted to her father, and that relationship is one of her primary motivations."

—MINNIE DRIVER

*Tarzan has been adapted to film many times over the years. It is second only to Dracula in movie adaptations.*

**A WITTY AND ENERGETIC VICTORIAN WITH A KEEN** sense of humor, Jane shares her father's interest in the environs and inhabitants of the African jungle. Neither xenophobic nor imperial, she has a great intellectual and emotional openness to the world that allows her to bond with Tarzan and his realm.

*Few but Jane can say: "I was saved by a flying wild man in a loincloth."*

# JIM HAWKINS

## THE FACTS

**NAME:** Jim Hawkins

**VOICED BY:** Joseph Gordon-Levitt

**DESCRIPTION:** Sensitive and good-hearted, boyishly handsome; also confused, hurt, and withdrawn

**SPECIAL SKILLS:** Solar surfing

**NOTE:** He's got the makings of greatness in him.

## CAREER

**FILMOGRAPHY:**
*Treasure Planet*, 2002

← *Academy graduation photo*

**A TRULY SWEET-NATURED BUT TROUBLED FIFTEEN-YEAR-** old, Jim is clever, loyal, and very loving to his mother, but suffers a great deal of teenage angst over the absence of his father, who walked out on the family when Jim was eight years old, leaving Jim devastated. The boy felt rejected and betrayed, and disappointed in himself for his perceived failure in the one thing he had worked hardest at: winning his father's love and approval.

Jim's anger made him withdrawn and sullen. He started failing at school, and his only method of escape, solar surfing, often put him in trouble with the authorities. His mother, Sarah, who has always tried to be supportive, now saw her son teetering on the verge of making some very bad choices.

The turning point in Jim's life came when a mysterious man named Billy Bones collapsed in the Benbow, Sarah Hawkins's inn, leaving Jim in possession of a map to the treasure of a thousand worlds. Soon Jim found himself on a dangerous adventure, sailing with a crew of pirates to planet where he would discover two priceless treasures: Captain Flint's hoard of gold, and, more importantly, self-confidence.

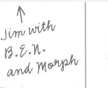

↑ *Jim with B.E.N. and Morph*

*About his mother: Cast unexpectedly into the role of single mother, Sarah is loving and accommodating, but upset by her son's behavior and worried about his future.*

# THE HUMAN TOUCH ▶ JOHN SILVER

*Treasure Planet was the first feature film simultaneously released to both regular and large-format (IMAX) theaters.*

## THE FACTS

**NAME:** John Silver

**VOICED BY:** Brian Murray

**FATHER:** Silver (like Jim) came from a broken home, grew up in conditions of poverty, and suffered from having an absent, uncaring father.

**SIDEKICK:** Silver's only true friend is his little proto-plasmic pet, Morph, whom he rescued from a dire situation; they've been inseparable ever since. Silver confides in Morph and, in some ways, Morph represents his conscience, his good side.

**DESCRIPTION:** Broad, theatrical, roguish, bear-like; a charming con man

## CAREER

**FILMOGRAPHY:**
*Treasure Planet*, 2002

↑ *Morph*

**CHARISMATIC SILVER IS BUILT LIKE A FORMER LINEBACKER WHO'S SEEN** better days. A cyborg (part man/part machine) with a mechanical arm, leg, and eye, he acts unschooled but is actually very smart. Silver intuitively knows people and their weaknesses. He has a great sense of humor, a twinkle in his eye, and is always ready with a good story. He learned early in life that he could use his charm to make anyone like him.

His mechanical arm has extraordinary strength and can transform into various useful tools. When cooking, his arm slices and dices, catches and breaks eggs, becomes a blowtorch, and makes julienne fries. As a pirate, he enjoys its more lethal functions, like transforming into a sword or a laser flintlock. His leg has a secret compartment that can turn into a cannon. His mechanical eye has telescopic vision, which can be used as a targeting mechanism and has the ability to scan objects and people.

In becoming something of a surrogate father to Jim, Silver wound up learning how to care about someone other than himself, ultimately causing him to go against his own grain and give up the treasure to save Jim's life. The bond that developed between them is one that can never be broken and one that changed each of them forever.

# THE BLUE FAIRY

### THE FACTS

**NAME:** Blue Fairy

**VOICED BY:** Evelyn Venable

**LIVE-ACTION MODEL:** Marge Belcher (Marge Champion)

**DESCRIPTION:** A lovely, ethereal blonde woman, clothed in diaphanous blue and comforting azure light, with a soothing and melodious voice

The live-action model for the Blue Fairy was Marge Belcher (also known as Marge Bell, Marge Babbitt, and finally, Marge Champion, of the famous dance duo Marge and Gower Champion). She had also modeled for the character of Snow White.

**THE BLUE FAIRY IS THE DRIVING FORCE BEHIND THE ENTIRE** *PINOCCHIO* story. As author John Grant notes, it is she who grants life to Pinocchio—twice—and appoints Jiminy Cricket as his "Official Conscience," and she acts as something of a guardian angel to both of them. Yet her origins and motives are never explicitly described—it is to be assumed that she is an ethereal being that is the embodiment of a wishful heart and a good spirit—or, as Grant summarized, "what the mysticists might call a 'principle.'"

**FROM THE DESK OF**

*Walt Disney*

Although she must give the appearance of loveliness, she can't look like a glamour girl.

Evelyn Venable, the voice of the Blue Fairy, was a model for the Columbia Pictures logo (the lady with the torch).

## CAREER

**FILMOGRAPHY:**
Pinocchio, 1940

The
BLUE FAIRY

TEMPORARY MODEL SHEET
FOR STORY DEP'T. USE
PINOCCHIO
J-3
© Walt Disney Prod.

Wings
are carried
transparent

NOTE
Feet and bottom
of robe blend out
as in large sketch.

## THE MAGIC TOUCH ▶ TINKER BELL

*In Sir James M. Barrie's original play, Tinker Bell is staged as a flying point of light, beamed from offstage.*

### THE FACTS

**NAME:** Tinker Bell

**LIVE ACTION MODEL:** Margaret Kerry

**SIGNIFICANT OTHER:** Peter and only Peter!

**DESCRIPTION:** Pretty, pouty, and protective—but ultimately good-hearted

**DOES NOT WORK WELL WITH:** Mermaids, Tiger Lily, Wendy

**TINKER BELL IS THE JEALOUS PIXIE THAT GLOWS BRIGHTEST FOR** Peter Pan. Her voice sings like a tinkling bell, and a sprinkle of her pixie dust can make you fly. But this sprite can turn spiteful if she suspects Peter's attentions are being diverted to anyone other than herself.

Tinker Bell went on to a second career as TV hostess for Disney's anthology series (*Disneyland*, *Walt Disney Presents*, *Walt Disney's Wonderful World of Color*, and *The Wonderful World of Disney*), and she still flies through the sky over several Disney theme parks to herald the evening fireworks.

## CAREER

**FILMOGRAPHY:**
Peter Pan, 1953
Return to Never Land, 2002

Tinkerball
Flesh Saddle 41
Hair
Dress  } Mustard 5
Shoes
Lips - Flame 4  To Carry
Eyebrows
Iris + Pupils ——— } Gray Blue 8
upper + lower Lashes
Ribbon - Lt. Green 3½ Henry
Make masks of Tink from Drawings.
Call FM1 to FM 14
Black Ink. FM
Wings on Sep. Cels. Call W Nos.
Surf 4 ink

STUDIO
CIRCULATION
ONLY

# FAIRY GODMOTHER

## THE FACTS

**NAME:** Fairy Godmother

**VOICED BY:** Verna Felton (1950); Russi Taylor (2002)

**DESCRIPTION:** Loving and wise; adept at transformations

**FAVORITE PHRASE:** "Bibbidi-Bobbidi-Boo!"

**WORKS WELL WITH:** Pumpkins, mice, dogs, horses

## CAREER

**FILMOGRAPHY:**
Cinderella, 1950
Cinderella II: Dreams Come True, 2002

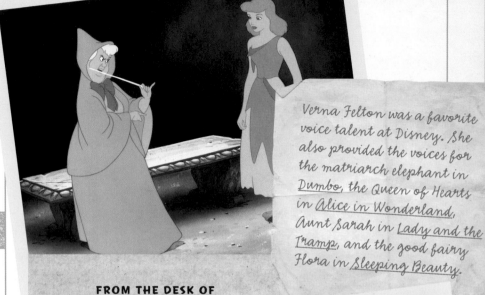

*Verna Felton was a favorite voice talent at Disney. She also provided the voices for the matriarch elephant in Dumbo, the Queen of Hearts in Alice in Wonderland, Aunt Sarah in Lady and the Tramp, and the good fairy Flora in Sleeping Beauty.*

*Legend has it that Walt Disney once told Marc Davis that the Fairy Godmother's transformation of Cinderella's rags into a shimmering ball gown was Walt's favorite piece of animation.*

### FROM THE DESK OF

## WALT DISNEY

The Fairy Godmother should have a kindly voice with a certain age in it. I don't see her as being goofy or stupid, but rather as having a wonderful sense of humor.

**A GRANDMOTHERLY SORCERESS, ROBED IN HUES OF** blue and accents of pink, the Fairy Godmother has a brief but all-important role in the story of Cinderella, performing the magical miracle that makes Cinderella's attendance at Prince Charming's Royal Ball possible. She is kind and funny, and the good cheer and confidence she gives to Cinderella are as important as her coach and slippers.

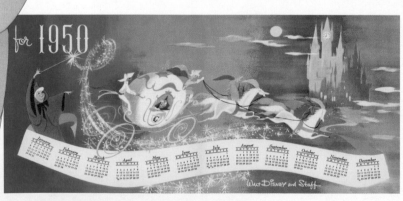

for 1950

Walt Disney and Staff

# THE MAGIC TOUCH ▶ FLORA, FAUNA, AND MERRYWEATHER

## THE FACTS

**NAMES:** Flora, Fauna, and Merryweather

**VOICED BY:** Verna Felton (Flora), Barbara Jo Allen (Fauna), Barbara Luddy (Merryweather)

**DESCRIPTION:** Three basic shapes: square (Flora), round (Merryweather), and triangular (Fauna); three basic colors: red (Flora), blue (Merryweather), and green (Fauna); three varied personalities.

## CAREER

**FILMOGRAPHY:**
*Sleeping Beauty,* 1959

*In initial development, Flora, Fauna, and Merryweather were designed to function according to their names. Flora was to have domain over the plants, Fauna over the animals, and Merryweather would control the climate. Walt ultimately discarded this notion, for although it offered many situations for humor, he felt that it led the overall story nowhere.*

*Throughout the history of man, three has been regarded as an almost mystical combination — Walt Disney recognized that a duo could offer contrast, but a <u>trio</u> offered a broad range of character interaction.*

**MOTHERLY, ECCENTRIC, MAGICAL, AND MORE THAN A BIT DAFT, THE THREE** fairies faithfully protected the Princess Aurora from the evil enchantment of wicked Maleficent. Hiding her in a cottage deep in the forest, they assumed the roles of her mortal "aunties" and for years and years hid her true identity from her.

## THE MAGIC TOUCH ▶ MERLIN

*He knows every trick in the book.*

### THE FACTS

**NAME:** Merlin

**VOICED BY:** Karl Swenson

**FAMILIAR:** Archimedes (an ill-tempered owl named after the Ancient Greek mathematician who said "Eureka!")

**DESCRIPTION:** Impatient and frequently befuddled, but with marvelous powers of magic, observation, and intellect

**NOTABLE QUOTE:** "Higitus Figitus migitus mum, pres-ti-dig-i-ton-i-um!"

### CAREER

**FILMOGRAPHY:**
*The Sword in the Stone*, 1963

**WITH HIS LONG WHITE BEARD, FLOWING** blue robes, and pointed cap, Merlin looks every bit the wizard famed in song and story. He is skilled at prestidigitation, transformation, transfiguration, enchantments, charms, and time travel. For all his intelligence and supernatural powers, he is often absent-minded, vexed, and annoyed.

## THE MAGIC TOUCH ▶ MADAM MIM

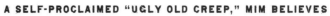

### THE FACTS

**NAME:** Madam Mim

**VOICED BY:** Martha Wentworth

**DESCRIPTION:** A cross between an aging spoiled brat and a young crotchety hag

### CAREER

**FILMOGRAPHY:**
*The Sword in the Stone*, 1963

*The Disney version of the Mim character was adopted into the comic book stories of Donald Duck, Mickey Mouse, and even Captain Hook. And in many European Disney comics, she is a good character!*

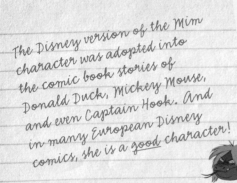

**A SELF-PROCLAIMED "UGLY OLD CREEP," MIM BELIEVES** herself to be the world's most talented and powerful wizard. She is egomaniacal, eccentric, and mercurial. Physically, she is heavy-set, busty, and nearly toothless, with poor posture to boot. When the call came to rescue Wart from Mim's clutches, Merlin challenged her to a sorcerer's duel in which the combatants transform into various animals. The duel (a treat to watch!) was nearly won by Mim when she dishonestly changed into a dragon, but Merlin made use of his micro-organism knowledge and transformed himself into a bacterium carrying a terrible disease, making Mim too ill to continue.

# THE MAGIC TOUCH ▶ GENIE

## THE FACTS

**NAME:** Genie

**VOICED BY:** Robin Williams; Dan Castellaneta (*The Return of Jafar*)

**DESCRIPTION:** Big, blue, bold, and a friend like no other

**SPECIAL SKILLS:** Wishes: three. No substitutions, exchanges, or refunds.

**NOTE:** Prefers to avoid tight spaces

Versatility is key to the Genie's performance. During his more than fifty magical transformations, he assumes the shape of (among other things):

- a Scotsman
- a Scottish terrier
- a slot machine
- a French maître d'
- a roast turkey
- a dragon
- a flight attendant
- a sheep
- a hammock
- Pinocchio
- a magician
- a goat
- a harem girl
- a talking lampshade
- a bee
- a submarine
- a one-man band
- a ventriloquist
- Jafar
- cheerleaders
- a baseball pitcher
- the moon

**FREED FROM A LIFETIME OF CONFINEMENT, GENIE RADIATES ENERGY** and geniality. Among (many) other functions, the wacky and wisecracking djinn provides a burst of slam-bang comedy. In his first encounter with Aladdin, he presented the youth with an incredibly fast-moving parade of verbal tricks, shape-shifting impersonations, and stand-up comedy routines, all while singing a rambunctious song—illustrating perfectly his impressive magical capabilities.

OFFICIAL DOCUMENTS

## CAREER

**FILMOGRAPHY:**
Aladdin, 1992
Aladdin: The Return
  of Jafar, 1994
Aladdin, 1994
  (TV series)
Aladdin and the King
  of Thieves, 1995

☑ HAT TOP
☐ LITE HILITE
■ DARK HILITE

SOLE
CANE TRIM
CANE TOP
SHOE
BELT
PANT
CANE
CLOSE LINE

The Genie owes his design
style to the intricate,
playful curlicue
of Persian miniatures,
as well as to the
distinctive flow and
curve of the drawings
of famed caricaturist
Al Hirschfeld.

The Genie was featured
as a summon in
the video game Kingdom
Hearts, in the level
named Agrabah.

# HUEY, DEWEY, AND LOUIE

## THE FACTS

**NAMES:** Huebert (Huey), Deuteronomy (Dewey), and Louis (Louie) Duck

**VOICE TALENT INCLUDES:** Clarence Nash (1934–1984); Tony Anselmo (*Disney's House of Mouse, Mickey Mouse Works*); Russi Taylor (1984–present)

**MOTHER:** Della (called Dumbella in the film "Donald's Nephews")

**OTHER CLOSE RELATIVES:** See *Donald Duck*

**DESCRIPTION:** Boys being boys—at full volume

**FAVORITE PHRASE:** "Hey, Unca Donald!"

**KNOWN ADVERSARIES:** The Beagle Boys; Witch Hazel & Beelzebub the Broom; Captain Ramrod & the Junior Chickadee Patrol; Flintheart Glomgold; Magica de Spell; Argus McSwine

**SPECIAL NOTE:** Also perform as The Quackstreet Boys

## CAREER

**FILMOGRAPHY:**
*DuckTales*, 1987 (TV series)
*DuckTales the Movie: Treasure of the Lost Lamp*, 1990
*Quack Pack*, 1996 (TV series)
*Mickey Mouse Works*, 1999 (TV series)
*Disney's House of Mouse*, 2001 (TV series)

**CARTOON APPEARANCES (HIGHLIGHTS):**
"Good Scouts," 1938
"Sea Scouts," 1939
"Donald's Snow Fight," 1942
"Donald's Happy Birthday," 1949
"Trick or Treat," 1949
"Spare the Rod," 1954

The names of the nephews were originally inspired by contemporary political figures Huey P. Long of Louisiana, Thomas E. Dewey of New York, and Louie Schmidt (friend of a Disney artist).

**HUEY, DEWEY, AND LOUIE ARE LIKE MINIATURE VERSIONS OF THEIR** uncle Donald—wound tighter (and louder), but with a lot more self-control. The siblings originally spent a good deal of time preying on the innate weaknesses of their short-fused "Unca." Later, they learned to focus their wild energy into more constructive channels, applying quick-witted assistance to the adventures of their uncles Donald and Scrooge McDuck. Much of their wisdom comes from their strict adherence to the rules, regulations, and teachings of the Junior Woodchucks.

# MORTY AND FERDIE, MAX GOOF

## THE FACTS

**NAMES:** Mortimer (Morty) and Ferdinand (Ferdie) Mouse

**VOICED BY:** Dick Billingsly was Morty (playing Tiny Tim) in *Mickey's Christmas Carol* (1983)

**MOTHER:** Mrs. Fieldmouse

**FAMOUS UNCLE:** Mickey Mouse

**PETS:** Pluto, Bianca the Goldfish, Milton the Siamese Cat, Leeza Belle the Cat

**DESCRIPTION:** Full of energy

## CAREER

**FILMOGRAPHY (HIGHLIGHTS):**
"Gulliver Mickey," 1934
*Mickey's House of Villains*, 2002

## MORTY AND FERDIE

**MINIATURIZED VERSIONS OF THEIR UNCLE**
Mickey, Morty and Ferdie first arrived when a Mrs. Fieldmouse (also called Amelia in Disney comics outside the United States) dropped them off at Mickey's house and asked him to take care of them while she ran an errand. The pair has always shown an appetite for adventure and a (sometimes foolishly) courageous spirit.

## THE FACTS

**NAME:** Maximillian Goof

**VOICED BY:**
Dana Hill (1992–1993);
Jason Marsden (current)

**SIGNIFICANT OTHER:** Roxanne

**FATHER:** Goofy

**MOTHER:** Unknown

**SIBLINGS:** Max bears some unknown relationship to the red-headed Goofy, Jr. from a series of short cartoons, including "Fathers Are People," 1951, and "Aquamania," 1961.

**DESCRIPTION:** Teenager to a *T*

## CAREER

**FILMOGRAPHY:**
*Goof Troop*, 1992
   (TV series)
*A Goofy Movie*, 1995
*An Extremely Goofy Movie*, 2000

## MAX GOOF

*Note: Works well with classmate PJ (Pete Jr.)*

**MAXIMILIAN "MAX" GOOF IS THE SON OF GOOFY. BY AND LARGE, HE'S** youthful, guileless, somewhat insecure, easily flustered, and (obviously) a little goofy—in other words, a typical teenage boy. He appeared (often wearing shades) in seventy-eight regular episodes of *Goof Troop*, as well as movies and specials. In *Disney's House of Mouse* he works as the parking valet.

Though Max is frequently heard groaning, "Awww, Dad!" and he's had to come to Goofy's rescue on more than one occasion, he remains a loyal kid who appreciates the bond he and his father share.

CHILDREN ▶ # ALICE

Lewis Carroll's <u>Alice's Adventures in Wonderland</u> (1865), and its sequel, <u>Through the Looking Glass</u> (1871), had fascinated Walt Disney since his youth.

## THE FACTS

**NAME:** Alice

**VOICED AND MODELED BY:** Kathryn Beaumont

**SIBLINGS:** A stern and practical sister

**CAT:** Dinah

**DESCRIPTION:** Pretty, petite; a curious and impatient dreamer

## CAREER

**FILMOGRAPHY:** *Alice in Wonderland*, 1951

*English artist David Hall presented an extensive storyboard development of the story in 1939. In 1943, another completely different set of storyboards was developed and presented.*

↑ *Tweedle-Dum and Tweedle-Dee confuse the issue.*

**ALICE IS A PRETTY BLONDE GIRL IN MARY-JANE SHOES, WHITE STOCKINGS,** and a blue pinafore with a white apron. Like many girls, she is tired of logic and lessons and ordinary life. She longs for a world where things are very different from the way they've always been.

That's why she was so very eager to follow the White Rabbit, despite some sound advice to herself about not going where one hasn't been invited. Once she tumbled in, it was too late to turn back, and Alice found Wonderland not only frustrating and per-plexing but as nonsensical and fantastical as she could have hoped.

Disney made several different announcements of <u>Alice in Wonderland</u> as a "forthcoming feature," and made many attempts to develop the story as a full-length film. Various well-known actresses were announced as live-action "Alices" to inhabit an animated Disney Wonderland.

Kathryn Beaumont, the young actress who voiced and modeled for Alice (as well as Wendy in <u>Peter Pan</u>), spent the majority of two years at the Walt Disney Studios, even going to school on the lot, so she could be on call for the duration of production.

Bread-and-butterflies!

# WENDY, MICHAEL, AND JOHN DARLING

## THE FACTS

**NAMES:** Wendy, Michael, and John Darling

**VOICED BY:** Kathryn Beaumont (Wendy), Tommy Luske (Michael), Paul Collins (John)

**SIGNIFICANT RELATIONSHIP:** Perhaps the most significant relationship of their young lives is their friendship with Peter Pan

**FATHER:** Mr. George Darling

**MOTHER:** Mrs. Mary Darling

**DOG:** Nana

**DESCRIPTION:** Young, perky, polite, and well-intentioned

## CAREER

**FILMOGRAPHY:**
*Peter Pan*, 1953
*Return to Never Land*, 2002
   (Wendy only)

**A FAMILY OF TYPICAL ENGLISH CHILDREN OF A CERTAIN TIME, THE** siblings are fully engaged in the world contained within the walls of their nursery. Wendy is still very much a child, but as the eldest is more than comfortable in adopting an attitude of maternity toward her two brothers, Peter Pan, and the Lost Boys.

John is the elder of the two boys, and cuts a rather dashing figure in his top hat; circular, thin-rimmed spectacles; and carefully-furled umbrella, trying very much to behave like a grown-up, but betrayed by his own youthful enthusiasm.

Michael is the youngest and smallest of the three Darling children. He cannot be separated, even in the direst circumstances, from his loyal teddy bear (or his pink pajamas).

*After the release of Peter Pan, Kathryn Beaumont resumed regular schooling and enrolled at the University of Southern California, where she earned a degree and teaching credential. Kathryn continued to work for the Walt Disney Studios each summer during college.*

"OH PETER, MY HERO!!"

<u>Peter Pan</u> was one of the first acting projects in the long career of English-born Paul Collins, who can still be seen in major motion pictures (<u>Dave</u>, <u>XXX: State of the Union</u>) and popular television series (<u>ER</u>, <u>The West Wing</u>, <u>Without a Trace</u>).

# ARTHUR, A.K.A. "WART"

## THE FACTS

**NAME:** Arthur

**NICKAME:** Wart

**VOICED BY:** Ricky Sorenson

**INSIGNIFICANT OTHER:**
A smitten lady squirrel

**FATHER:** Sir Ector, Master
of the Castle of the Forest
Sauvage (foster father)

**SIBLINGS:** Sir Kay (foster
brother)

**TUTOR:** Merlin the magician

**DESCRIPTION:** Subservient;
physically unimpressive

**SPECIAL SKILL:** Shape-shifting
(with help from Merlin)

## CAREER

**FILMOGRAPHY:**
*The Sword in the Stone*, 1963

*Wart and Merlin →*

*← Easy does it . . .*

**SKINNY AND UNDERSIZED, WITH A MOP OF LIGHT BLOND HAIR AND AN**
ill-fitting rough tunic, eleven-year-old Arthur certainly seems to fit his nickname
of "Wart."

In Wart's time a great tournament was held in London on New Year's Day
to pick the new king. Wart, attending as Kay's squire, forgot Kay's sword and ran
back to the inn to get it, only to find the inn locked. So Wart, seeing the sword
in the stone, innocently—and
easily (destiny is that way)—
pulled it out.

When the knights mar-
veled at the wondrous sword
and questioned where he got
it, Wart had to prove himself

*The songs for The Sword in the Stone, including*
*"A Most Befuddling Thing," "That's What*
*Makes the World Go Round," "Higitus Figitus,"*
*and "The Legend of the Sword in the Stone,"*
*were written by Disney songwriting legends*
*Richard M. and Robert B. Sherman.*

*↑*
*Wart and Archimedes*

Sir Ector and Wart

**WHIZ-BANG WHIZARD of WHIMSY!**

Tired of living in a Medieval mess...
Merlin uses all his
magic powers to change a
scrawny boy into a
legendary hero!

STILL ONLY 12¢

**WALT DISNEY'S**

NEWEST AND MOST HILARIOUS ALL-CARTOON FEATURE

The *Sword*
in the *Stone*

Story by BILL PEET · Based on the book by T. H. WHITE · Released by BUENA VISTA Distribution Co., Inc. · © 1963 Walt Disney Productions

...TS THE DRAGON IN THE DAYS OF THE KNIGHTS

*Two songs written for the film but scrapped before production began were "The Blue Oak Tree" and "The Magic Key". The latter was to be Merlin's lecture to Arthur about the value of an education. It was replaced with "Higitus Figitus."*

all over again, and he pulled the sword from the stone one more time—and was proclaimed king by the marveling warriors. As king, Arthur was apprehensive of his ability to rule, but luckily Merlin returned to reassure him.

An underdog without a will of his own, he hardly appeared to be royal material. Readying Wart for his destined ascension to the throne of England required all of the effort the great Merlin could muster—but by being changed into various animals by the magician, Wart learned the basic truths of life.

Wart with Merlin

CHILDREN ▶ # MOWGLI

Throughout his career, Walt Disney was on the lookout for great stories to bring to life. Rudyard Kipling's 1894 classic <u>The Jungle Book</u> first caught Walt's attention in the late 1930s; he finally acquired the film rights in 1962.

## THE FACTS

**NAME:** Mowgli

**ALSO KNOWN AS:** Man-cub

**VOICED BY:** Bruce Reitherman (1967); Haley Joel Osment (2003)

**SIGNIFICANT OTHER:** Shanti (the village girl)

**MOTHER(S):** Raksha (the wolf); Messua (the human)

**DESCRIPTION:** Determined, stubborn

**WORKS WELL WITH:** Baloo, Bagheera

**DOES NOT WORK WELL WITH:** Kaa, Shere Khan, King Louie

## CAREER

**FILMOGRAPHY:**
*The Jungle Book*, 1967
*The Jungle Book 2*, 2003

**RAISED BY A WOLF PACK, ALL TEN-YEAR-OLD MOWGLI WANTED WAS** to stay in the jungle. But after Shere Khan, the tiger who hates all men, vowed to kill him, Mowgli's friends Bagheera, the panther, and Baloo, his adopted "papa bear," resolved to take this man-cub to the man-village before it was too late. Along the way, Mowgli searched for a place to belong, adopting the life of an elephant, a bear, a monkey, even a vulture...but unfortunately, these new friends often proved more dangerous than sincere. Though he was initially angry with Bagheera and Baloo for trying to take him from the jungle, Mowgli soon learned that friends are the ones who tell you what you need to hear—even if it's not what you *want* to hear.

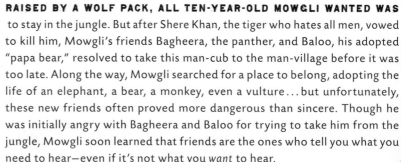

*Friends like Baloo make life more bear-able.*

The Jungle is JUMPIN'!

WALT DISNEY presents

# The Jungle Book

Sebastian CABOT "Bagheera" the Panther · Louis PRIMA "King Louie" the Ape · George SANDERS "Shere Khan" the Tiger · Sterling HOLLOWAY "Kaa" the Snake

The Jungle Book was the last animated feature that Walt Disney personally supervised. He died during its production, and there was a lot of worry about whether the Disney Animation Staff could make the film work without Walt. But when it was released, The Jungle Book was a blockbuster hit. Its winning combination of captivating characters, humor, drama, and music has made it one of Disney's most beloved animated features.

↑
Shanti

CHILDREN ▶ # PENNY

_Oliver & Company_ was originally intended as a sequel to _The Rescuers_, with Penny as the little girl who adopts the orphan kitten. Ultimately, Penny was changed to Jenny, and the few connections between the films were dropped.

## THE FACTS

**NAME:** Penny

**VOICED BY:** Michelle Stacy

**SIDEKICK:** Teddy

**DESCRIPTION:** Sweet, sad, brave, hopeful

## CAREER

**FILMOGRAPHY:**
The Rescuers, 1977

**PENNY IS A YOUNG ORPHAN GIRL WITH LIGHT BROWN HAIR TIED IN A** short bunch at the back. Her soulful blue eyes are matched by her blue-gray tunic and light blue blouse. She was kidnapped by wicked Madame Medusa because she was small enough to fit into the hiding place of The Devil's Eye diamond. Medusa also used Penny's beloved teddy bear as both a threat against the girl and a hiding place for the diamond.

Besides her Teddy, Penny gets sound guidance from a wise old cat named Rufus, who helped Bernard and Bianca glean the identity of Madame Medusa.

CHILDREN ▶ # CODY

## THE FACTS

**NAME:** Cody

**VOICED BY:** Adam Ryen

**SIDEKICK:** Field operative Jake the Kangaroo Rat

**DESCRIPTION:** Brave, dynamic, devoted; a young man of action and integrity

## CAREER

**FILMOGRAPHY:**
*The Rescuers Down Under,* 1990

*Adam Ryen, the boy who voiced Cody, also dubbed the character in his native Norwegian.*

**AN EIGHT-YEAR-OLD OUTBACK LAD** with tousled hair, a lithe build, and physical agility, Cody has committed himself to saving animals being ensnared and endangered by poachers—putting himself directly in the cross-hairs of the villain McLeach. A call for help to the Rescue Aid Society brought intrepid mice Bernard and Bianca to his aid.

## A NOTE FROM
# JOHN GRANT,
### AUTHOR

Cody is . . . a brilliant accomplishment. Time and again, adult viewers remarked that the most striking thing about *The Rescuers Down Under* was that Cody was "a real boy."

# LILO PELEKAI

*← Lilo & Nani*

## THE FACTS

**NAME:** Lilo Pelekai

**VOICED BY:** Daveigh Chase

**SIBLING:** Nani Pelekai (sister/guardian)

**DESCRIPTION:** Cute, smart, and lively—but rendered friendless, dejected, ostracized, and sad by her circumstances

## CAREER

**FILMOGRAPHY:**
*Lilo & Stitch*, 2002
*Stitch! The Movie*, 2003
*Lilo & Stitch: The Series*, 2003
  (TV series)
*Lilo & Stitch 2:*
  *Stitch Has a Glitch*, 2005

*Etymological Note:*

*The name "Lilo" means "Generous One," and its origin is Hawaiian. It can also be interpreted as "Lost"; this would give the song title "He Mele No Lilo" a loose translation as "Lullaby of the Lost."*

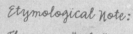

**LILO IS A HAWAIIAN GIRL WHO LIVES WITH HER NINETEEN-YEAR-OLD** sister/guardian, Nani. The two girls are struggling to make it on their own, and things aren't going particularly well. Lilo tends to have a hard time making friends, and her maturity and taste are out of step with other kids her age. But in the end, her appreciation for Elvis Presley, and her love, faith, and unwavering belief in *'ohana* (the Hawaiian word and concept for family) helped Lilo and her new "dog," Stitch, find their way "home."

Overseeing the animation for the title character, Lilo, was twenty-year Disney veteran Andreas Deja, considered one of the world's top animators.

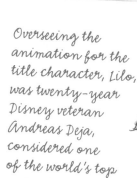

## NANI PELEKAI

**VOICED BY:** Tia Carrere

NANI, LILO'S NINETEEN-YEAR-OLD SISTER, BECAME her guardian after the death of their parents in a car crash. Though the two girls often butt heads, Nani truly wants what's best for Lilo, and tried to help them both find happiness while preventing social worker Cobra Bubbles from tearing them apart.

## DAVID KAWENA

**VOICED BY:** Jason Scott Lee

DAVID IS NANI'S BOYFRIEND. AN AVID SURFER, HE taught the Pelekais how to ride the waves and supported Nani as she learned the ropes of raising her sister—and coped with the knowledge of Stitch's alien identity.

### A NOTE FROM
# DEAN DEBLOIS,
#### CO-DIRECTOR

Lilo is, in a way, the constant that other things bend around. She's the one that doesn't swerve, no matter what happens to her. She always believes in family and holds onto that belief. She knows better than any of the other characters that family isn't so much a *thing* as it is an *idea*.

# PETER PAN

## THE FACTS

**NAME:** Peter Pan

**VOICED BY:** Bobby Driscoll (1953); Blayne Weaver (2002)

**LIVE-ACTION MODELS:** Bobby Driscoll; Roland Dupree

**SIGNIFICANT OTHERS:** Wendy Darling, Tinker Bell, Tiger Lily

**DESCRIPTION:** Charming, brave, uncomplicated, joyous

**WORKS WELL WITH:** Mermaids, Indians, Lost Boys, the Crocodile

**DOES NOT WORK WELL WITH:** Pirates, Captain Hook, adults in general

### FROM THE DESK OF

## Walt Disney

He flies without wings. His shadow leads a merry little life of its own. Face-to-face with the terrible Captain Hook, Peter dispatches that pirate with jaunty ease. Peter is at home with mermaids and understands their language. He is twelve years old forever simply because he refuses to grow up beyond that comfortable age. Most remarkable of all, he knows where Never Land is and how to get there.

**PETER PAN IS THE VERY SPIRIT OF YOUTH,** traveling from the enchanted isle of Never Land all the way to London just to hear Wendy Darling spin tales about him and his adventures. While his ego may seem inflated at times, even his arch-nemesis, Captain Hook, knows that Pan's no ordinary boy. He can fly without wings and match Hook's cutlass with nothing more than a dagger. He's also the un-disputed leader of the Lost Boys, and allows no break in the ranks. Time makes little difference to him; when you never grow up, life is nothing but fun, whimsy, and adventure.

*The original little boy who won't grow up!*

PETER PAN DESCRIBES NEVER
LAND TO KIDS IN NURSERY
... BUILDING UP
... CLIMAX WITH MUSIC
... ARE SO...

## CAREER

**FILMOGRAPHY:**
Peter Pan, 1953
Return to Never Land, 2002

The casting of a male actor in the part of Disney's _Peter Pan_ was especially significant, since Sir James M. Barrie's original stage play featured an adult woman in the role. This became a theatrical tradition that remained unbroken until Walt Disney's animated feature was released.

NO. 446
**Walt Disney's**
**CAPTAIN HOOK**
**and Peter Pan**

PERPETUAL CHILDREN: Peter Pan

VILLAINS ▶  # KAA

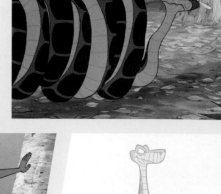

## THE FACTS

**NAME:** Kaa

**VOICED BY:** Sterling Holloway (1967); Jim Cummings (current)

**DESCRIPTION:** Spellbinding personality, slick behavior

**METHOD OF MENACE:** Hypnosis and powerful coils

**SPECIAL NOTE:** *NEVER* engage him in an eye-staring contest

## CAREER

**FILMOGRAPHY:**
*The Jungle Book*, 1967
*Jungle Cubs*, 1996
   (TV series)
*Mickey's House of Villains*, 2002
*The Jungle Book 2*, 2003

*Generally, pythons like Kaa range in size from fifteen to twenty feet in length. They are among the longest species of snake in the world.*

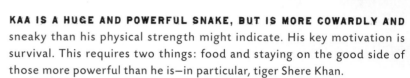

**KAA IS A HUGE AND POWERFUL SNAKE, BUT IS MORE COWARDLY AND** sneaky than his physical strength might indicate. His key motivation is survival. This requires two things: food and staying on the good side of those more powerful than he is—in particular, tiger Shere Khan.

He does possess a certain capacity for mesmerizing eye contact. In the past he has hypnotized man-cub Mowgli, once while hypnotizing Bagheera as well, and again while seductively singing his slithery entreaty, "Trust in Me."

A reviewer once wrote about the snake, "Not the most fear-inspiring villain, he definitely makes an impression as the cunning type...Kaa is a likable villain, namely because his own pride gets in the way of him actually doing anything truly evil."

First introduced in the story "Kaa's Hunting" in Rudyard Kipling's *The Jungle Book*, Kaa is more than a hundred years old and still in his prime. In the tale, Bagheera and Baloo enlist his help to rescue Mowgli when the boy is captured by the Bandar-log (monkeys) and taken to an abandoned human city. Kaa breaks down the wall of the building in which Mowgli is imprisoned and uses his serpentine hypnosis to draw the monkeys toward his waiting jaws. Bagheera and Baloo are also entranced, but in the story, Mowgli is immune because he is human and breaks the spell on his friends.

# VILLAINS ▶ SHERE KHAN

## THE FACTS

**NAME:** Shere Khan

**VOICED BY:** George Sanders (1967); Jason Marsden (1996); Tony Jay (1990 and 2003)

**DESCRIPTION:** Physically sturdy and graceful; a feline beauty with fierce strength

**SPECIAL SKILLS:** Excellent sneer

**METHOD OF MENACE:** Physical intimidation, suave intellect, ominous claws

## CAREER

**FILMOGRAPHY:**
*The Jungle Book*, 1967
*TaleSpin*, 1990
   (TV series)
*Jungle Cubs*, 1996
   (TV series)
*The Jungle Book 2*, 2003

*Shere Khan is named after a Pashtun prince (Sher Khan Nasher) Rudyard Kipling encountered on his trips to Afghanistan.*

**SHERE KHAN IS A STEALTHY AND SINISTER JUNGLE CAT, EXTREMELY** powerful, clever—and deadly. His mere presence in the jungle compelled the wolf pack to send Mowgli away, since Shere Khan would gladly kill the boy just because he's human. The only things this cat fears are fire and guns.

Shere Khan is the chief villain in two of Rudyard Kipling's *Jungle Book* stories featuring Mowgli. Despite being born with a withered leg—and derisively nicknamed "Lungri" (the Lame One) by his own mother—Shere Khan is aggressive and arrogant, and regards himself as the rightful lord of the jungle. The only creature that looks up to him, however, is the despised and cowardly jackal Tabaqui.

# LADIES-IN-HATING

## THE FACTS

**NAME:** Queen of Hearts

**VOICED BY:** Verna Felton

**SIGNIFICANT OTHER:** King of Hearts (a rather effete and henpecked ruler, whose timorous demeanor is perfectly suited to the needs of his spouse)

**DESCRIPTION:** Colossal carriage and imperial egocentricity

**FAVORITE PHRASE:** "Off with their heads!"

**SPECIAL SKILLS:** Stylish wardrobe; exceptional at croquet

**METHOD OF MENACE:** Intimidation, monarchic will, and volume

**SPECIAL NOTE:** Requires anger management and sensitivity training

## CAREER

**FILMOGRAPHY:**
*Alice in Wonderland*, 1951

### A NOTE FROM
### KRAM NEBUER,
**ULTIMATED DISNEY.COM,**
*THE TOP DISNEY
VILLAIN COUNTDOWN*

One word: psycho.

## QUEEN OF HEARTS

CONFIDENTIAL

**WITH THE GRACE OF MOVEMENT OF A GIGANTIC OCEAN LINER PLYING THE** sea, the Queen of Hearts is an elegant yet imposing monarch who lacks the polish of most royal matrons. She tends to be childish and irresponsible, irrational and unpredictable—personality flaws that rarely affect her, since she is the ultimate authority in her realm.

## THE FACTS

**NAME:** Yzma

**VOICED BY:** Eartha Kitt

**PARTNER-IN-CRIME:** For now, Kronk (handsome, athletic, and a gifted epicure; not terribly bright, but speaks fluent squirrel)

**DESCRIPTION:** Lanky, shrill, skeletal, pale—and very, very, very, very old

**SPECIAL TALENTS:** Potions and poisons

**METHOD OF MENACE:** Sorcery, science, and fear tactics

## CAREER

**FILMOGRAPHY:**
*The Emperor's New Groove,* 2000
*Kronk's New Groove,* 2005
*The Emperor's New School,* 2006
   (TV series)

# YZMA

*By the looks of it, mascara came into vogue long before teeth whitening.*

**THIS DEVIOUS DIVA WAS A GAMINE** beauty—a *long* time ago. She has an ultra-long neck, very bony hips and shoulders, and extremely long arms—all of which were probably willowy and lovely . . . last century.

*Yzma owes much of her distinctive style to artist Joe Moshier, who chose to emphasize bold straights, confident curves, and clear silhouettes. "Yzma is very skeletal with big oval eyes," Moshier says. "Her anatomy is also a bit outrageous; we really exaggerated her hips . . . It was a lot of fun designing her clothes."*

## THE FACTS

**NAME:** Madame Medusa

**VOICED BY:** Geraldine Page

**PETSY-POOS:** Crocodiles Nero and Brutus

**PARTNER-IN-CRIME:** Mr. Snoops

**DESCRIPTION:** Hennaed hair, frowsy dress, loping gait

**FAVORITE PHRASE:** "Find that big diamond!"

**METHOD OF MENACE:** Threats, shouts, screams, shrieks, and mild violence

## CAREER

*In an unprecedented Disney animation casting decision, the role of The Rescuers' principal baddie was originally assigned to veteran villainess Cruella De Vil. In the end, it was decided that this would only result in unwanted comparisons between the films, and the idea was scratched.*

# MADAME MEDUSA

**OVERWHELMING, AUTHORITATIVE, AND ENTERTAINING, WITH THE LOOKS,** cynical worldview, and wardrobe of an over-the-hill chanteuse, Medusa has a heart blacker than the murky waters of the Devil's Bayou. As owner of Madame Medusa's Pawnshop Boutique, she must have the Devil's Eye—and won't rest until she clutches that glittery diamond in her greedy palms.

Her plan in the 1977 film *The Rescuers* was simple: find a child—a skinny, homely child that no one would miss—and drop it into the watery cave where the elusive diamond resided. She knew she could handle a child with her patented mixture of sickly sweet cajoling and evil threats. With the ungainly Mr. Snoops as her partner-in-crime, she found little Penny and had no compunction about abandoning her to whatever fate had in store. Never did she suspect that a pair of brave mice would foil her plans!

← *Nero and Brutus*

# MEN OF MEANS

## THE FACTS

**NAME:** Gaston

**VOICED BY:** Richard White

**SIGNIFICANT OTHER:** Himself, though his goal is to marry Belle

**DESCRIPTION:** Tall, dark, and handsome; also, boorish, arrogant, and violent

**CO-STAR COMMENT:** "Gaston is positively primeval." (Belle)

**METHOD OF MENACE:** Physical superiority, threat of bodily harm, skillful use of firearms

## CAREER

**FILMOGRAPHY:**
*Beauty and the Beast*, 1991
"Beauty and the Beast," 1994 (Theatrical show)

## GASTON

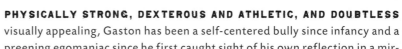

**PHYSICALLY STRONG, DEXTEROUS AND ATHLETIC, AND DOUBTLESS** visually appealing, Gaston has been a self-centered bully since infancy and a preening egomaniac since he first caught sight of his own reflection in a mirror. In other words, he's a book that should not be judged by its cover.

Incensed after Belle refused to marry him (because how could she refuse a man who prides himself on his expectorating capabilities?), he cooked up a scheme that involved throwing her father in an asylum and leading a raid on the Beast's castle. Positively dastardly!

# RATIGAN

*Note: Ratigan voice talent Vincent Price is a legend on the horror movie circuit, having played a host of evil characters in his long career, but his only other role for Disney was in the 1982 film* <u>Vincent</u>.

**PROFESSOR RATIGAN IS A MAD GENIUS WHO DWELLS IN SPLENDOR** beneath the streets of London, with a gaggle of cowering lackeys to sing his praises, light his cigarettes, and cater to his every evil whim. He's only got one problem: mouse detective Basil of Baker Street, his oh-so-clever nemesis. Theirs is the greatest rivalry ever to exist between criminal and detective.

Demented mastermind that he is, Ratigan believed he could tip the balance in his own favor, forcing all of Mousedom to cower at his little feet. But his ambitions ultimately proved bigger than his powers.

# GOVERNOR RATCLIFFE

**RATCLIFFE BEARS AN IMPOSING AND TOWERING FRAME, TOPPED BY A** rather pointed head. His face is prim and foppish, complete with a moustache and imperial beard. He's quite the snappy dresser for a man infiltrating the wilds of the New World.

Like so many desperate men throughout history, Governor Ratcliffe has been completely consumed by the dream of gold. His obsession with riches and the power they bring has made him utterly selfish, mean, and violent. His monomania fits well with his xenophobia (go find a dictionary).

# MEAN MEN

## THE FACTS

**NAME:** Lyle Tiberius Rourke

**VOICED BY:** James Garner

**PARENTS:** Lt. Col. Jackson and Rachel Lee Rourke

**A LIFETIME OF SERVICE:** Joined U.S. Army in July 1875; served through 1901

**DESCRIPTION:** Pragmatic, tough, and mercenary; makes his own rules

**METHOD OF MENACE:** Military discipline, physical superiority

## CAREER

**FILMOGRAPHY:**
*Atlantis: The Lost Empire*, 2001

## LYLE T. ROURKE

**LYLE T. ROURKE LEARNED THE WAYS OF MILITARY LIFE AT AN EARLY AGE** when his father, a cavalry officer, was killed in battle. After repeated expulsions from boarding school for fighting, Rourke resolved to follow in his father's footsteps and joined the military at fifteen. There, he exhibited a remarkable talent for leadership, owing to his analytical mind and charisma. He married in June of 1887, but his wife left him after only four months. Rourke, a pragmatist both personally and professionally, tends to take what he needs and discard anything he considers "useless baggage."

He helmed numerous expeditions during his career, most notably leading the Whitmore Expedition to Atlantis.

## THE FACTS

**NAME:** Judge Claude Frollo

**VOICED BY:** Tony Jay

**DESCRIPTION:** Self-righteous, uncaring, loathsome

**METHOD OF MENACE:** Fear and force

## CAREER

**FILMOGRAPHY:**
*The Hunchback of Notre Dame*, 1996

## JUDGE FROLLO

**THE ULTIMATE AUTHORITY FIGURE, JUDGE CLAUDE FROLLO RULES PARIS** with a cruel hand. He seeks to destroy the Gypsies, but he cannot destroy the spirit that burns within Notre Dame's hunchbacked bell-ringer, Quasimodo, for whom Frollo acts as a reluctant and repressive guardian.

An unusual Disney villain in that he seeks neither wealth nor power (because he already possesses both), Frollo has a rare sophistication, which he expected would help him gain the affections of a certain beautiful Gypsy woman. But in the end, his obsession for control proved to be his downfall.

## PERCIVAL C. McLEACH

With Joanna ↙

**NAME:** Percival C. McLeach

**VOICED BY:** George C. Scott

**SIGNIFICANT OTHER:** Joanna (a vicious but cowardly lizard with a fondness for eggs)

**DESCRIPTION:** Brutal, ruthless

**METHOD OF MENACE:** Physical intimidation, kidnapping, imprisonment, torture

**CAREER**

**FILMOGRAPHY:**
*The Rescuers Down Under,* 1990

**THE EVIL POACHER McLEACH BELIEVES IN "RECYCLING" ENDANGERED** animals into purses and wallets. With his giant bushwhacker machine, he tears up the countryside, catching whatever wildlife falls into his snares. The prize he covets most is the great golden eagle Marahute and her eggs. He'll use every trick he knows to catch and kill her—going as far as kidnapping a young boy in hopes of finding her secret hideaway.

## CECIL CLAYTON

OFFICIAL DOCUMENTS

**THE FACTS**

**NAME:** Cecil Clayton

**VOICED BY:** Brian Blessed

**DESCRIPTION:** Brawny, bright, deceitful, disloyal

**METHOD OF MENACE:** Threats, physical treachery, firearms

**FIENDISH DESIRE:** "I was created for Africa and Africa was created for me!"

**CAREER**

**FILMOGRAPHY:**
*Tarzan,* 1999
*Tarzan,* 2003
  (TV series)

**SUAVE AND DUPLICITOUS, CLAYTON IS A SWAGGERING BIG GAME HUNTER** and adventurer. He's bigger than life and boisterous, but there's a hidden meaning in his words; he is not at all what he appears to be. Clayton thrives on being in control of a situation and really feels at home in the wilderness. A total egomaniac, he has enjoyed a lifelong romance—with himself. (He *adores* himself.) He's a tremendous foe, physically intimidating and clever, and comfortable in the jungle environs.

EXTRA-EVIL
VILLAINS ▶ # THE QUEEN

## THE FACTS

**NAME:** The Queen

**ALIAS:** Peddler Woman

**VOICED BY:** Lucille LaVerne

**SIGNIFICANT OTHER:** The King
(Snow White's father), deceased

**HENCHMAN:** A greasy black raven

**DESCRIPTION:** Coldly beautiful
and heartlessly vain, with a
serene and unfeeling face

**WORKS WELL WITH:**
Mirrors, cauldrons, potions,
ravens, spells

**DOES NOT WORK WELL WITH:**
Forest animals, pursuing dwarfs

**FAVORITE PHRASE:** "Magic
Mirror on the wall, who is the
fairest one of all?"

**METHOD OF MENACE:**
Evil spells and potions;
magic mirror

### A NOTE FROM
# FRANK AND OLLIE,
#### VILLAINS DEPT.

Both the wicked Queen and the
Peddler Woman turned
out to be more frightening
than Walt Disney anticipated:
He never made another
villain that scary, that
real, that menacing.

**THE QUEEN'S SOLE MOTIVATION IS PHYSICAL BEAUTY AND HER ABILITY**
to maintain it. Her evil and hatred come from nothing more than her fiend-
ishly obsessive desire to remain the "fairest in the land" (no matter that Snow
White is innocent and harmless).

A PERFECT DISGUISE

**FILMOGRAPHY:**
*Snow White and the Seven Dwarfs*, 1937

## FROM THE DESK OF
# WALT DISNEY

A mixture of Lady Macbeth and
the Big Bad Wolf—her beauty is
sinister, mature, plenty of
curves—she becomes ugly and
menacing when scheming and
mixing her poisons—magic
fluids transform her into an
old, witch-like hag.

PRODUCTION F.I
"SNOW WHITE"
WITCH MODEL

FEB. 25 1937    © 1937    SHEET 1
W.D.P.

-----BY HER WICKED STEP-
MOTHER, THE QUEEN!

# LADY TREMAINE

## THE FACTS

**NAME:** Lady Tremaine

**VOICED/MODELED BY:** Eleanor Audley (1950); Susan Blakeslee (voice, 2002)

**HENCHMAN:** Lucifer (a fat, lazy, spoiled cat with his mistress's meaner qualities)

**RELATIVES:** Anastasia and Drizella (daughters); Cinderella (stepdaughter)

**DESCRIPTION:** Icy smile, rigid poise, extreme self-control

**METHOD OF MENACE:** Cruelty, treachery, dishonesty, absolute control

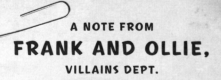

### A NOTE FROM
## FRANK AND OLLIE,
#### VILLAINS DEPT.

There was hardly a moment when the Stepmother was not running something through her mind, constantly scheming, which made her such a menace. Her piercing, penetrating eyes gave a look of intense concentration.

**A WOMAN OF GOOD FAMILY AND STATELY** elegance, Lady Tremaine lives by the maxims "above all, self-control" and "you must always keep your word." Therefore, Cinderella's wicked stepmother cunningly chooses her words with care and—unlike her awkward daughters—never lets her temper get the best of her. She is well dressed and impeccably groomed, and her comportment and etiquette are above reproach.

Cinderella's widowed father chose this widow of gentle birth because he thought he was protecting his daughter's future welfare. But with his passing, a great change came over the stepmother. Lady Tremaine carefully cultivated a patronizing dignity, a thin mask for her innate severity and cruelty.

Her complete selfishness engendered a remarkable talent for deviousness and manipulation. While she realizes that Anastasia and Drizella are clumsy, unattractive, spoiled, and charmless, she nevertheless views her daughters as a means to her own status and wealth.

Lady Tremaine has no magic powers and lacks flamboyance, which oddly makes her one of the most frightening of villains, because she is purely human—and purely evil.

# ANASTASIA AND DRIZELLA

**VOICED BY:** Lucille Bliss (Anastasia),
Rhoda Elaine Williams (Drizella)

**SPOILED, AWKWARD, AND UNGAINLY, BUT WITH A REMARKABLY** high opinion of themselves, the two sisters are easily carried away by jealousy and power. Bickering constantly, they love to blame everything on poor Cinderella, spitefully working their beautiful stepsister to the bone at chores they're "too good" to perform while idling their time away in bed or fussing with their hair. Not entirely blind to their shortcomings, their mother does her best to instill in them a sense of elegance and style, but even with instruction in music and decorum, the sisters hardly sing like nightingales or look like swans. Still, each firmly believes that she is a bride fit for a prince.

# CAPTAIN HOOK

## THE FACTS

**NAME:** Captain Hook (first name may be John or James)

**VOICED BY:** Hans Conried (1953); Corey Burton (current)

**LIVE-ACTION MODELS:** Hans Conried, Henry Brandon

**HENCHMAN:** Mr. Smee

**DESCRIPTION:** Flamboyant, disreputable, malevolent

**WORKS WELL WITH:** Pistols, swords, Smee

**DOES NOT WORK WELL WITH:** Sailors, pirates, mermaids, Lost Boys, fairies, Indians, crocodiles

**SPECIAL SKILL:** Piano playing

**METHOD OF MENACE:** Unfailing pursuit of revenge

**CAPTAIN HOOK IS A PIRATE WITH A GRUDGE. HE FANCIES HIMSELF TOO** clever for an impudent imp like Peter Pan—though in their last bout, the boy fed Hook's hand to the Crocodile. Dead-set on revenge, Hook and his ship and all its men will stay anchored in Never Land's waters until he gets it.

Yet, like most bullies, Hook is a coward—especially when it comes to the Crocodile. This creature poses no harm to anyone else; he's as intent on getting Hook as Hook is on getting Pan. The beast has already ingested Hook's left hand and will forever hunger for more. (At least his motives are as unambiguous as his behavior.)

The Captain loves to play at refinement and gentlemanly pursuits—fine dining, fine wines, and fine music—but he is at heart a scoundrel who thinks nothing of drowning Indian Princess Tiger Lily to get at Peter Pan, or imprisoning the delicate pixie Tinker Bell for the same ends.

Hook has even turned his handicap into an opportunity to be fashionable, accumulating a shiny array of hooks and appendages for all occasions. (All this does make one wonder what his name was *before* the Crocodile ate his hand.)

**FILMOGRAPHY:**
Peter Pan, 1953
Mickey's House of Villains, 2002
Return to Never Land, 2002

# MR. SMEE

**VOICED BY:** Bill Thompson (1953);
Jeff Bennett (2002)

**A LOYAL FIRST MATE TO CAPTAIN HOOK, SMEE** desperately wishes to give up his boss's vain quest for revenge against Peter Pan—which may be the smartest idea ever to echo in his thick skull. Smee's true following is following Hook's orders. He'll happily do anything for his "Cap'n," even tie Tiger Lily to an anchor to drown her at high tide. Obviously dangerous in his efforts to please, he's sometimes even a threat to Hook himself. (Nailing a DO NOT DISTURB sign outside the captain's cabin, he unknowingly hammered the tyrant senseless.)

87109-1

# MALEFICENT

The name "maleficent" cleverly combines "malice" and "malevolent."

## THE FACTS

**NAME:** Maleficent

**VOICED BY:** Eleanor Audley (1959); Lois Nettleton (2002)

**HENCHMAN:** Diablo (a sleek, graceful black raven)

**DESCRIPTION:** Aloof, chic, striking; capable of strong entrances and exits

**WORKS WELL WITH:** Goons

**DOES NOT WORK WELL WITH:** Good fairies

**SPECIAL SKILL:** Shape-shifting

**CO-STAR COMMENT:** "Maleficent doesn't know anything about love, or kindness, or the joy of helping others. You know, sometimes I really don't think she's very happy." (Flora)

*It appears that Maleficent may have once enjoyed a position in King Stefan's court and is now an outcast.*

*It is safe to assume that Maleficent, Flora, Fauna, and Merryweather have a past together, although what it is exactly is never revealed.*

**MALEFICENT IS OFTEN CITED AS ONE OF THE FAVORITE DISNEY VILLAINS,** but she is a triumph of style over substance. She uses her strong presence to keep people at a distance, so they won't realize that she has no emotional core and lacks self-esteem. Her incentives are neither very clear nor very rational. In essence, she is an angry loner, but she has spent a large portion of her life in a snit because she didn't get invited to a social event—Princess Aurora's royal sanctification.

Maleficent must be *seen* to feel significant, so not receiving the invitation to Aurora's first court appearance was a slight that cut her quite deeply.

While on the proverbial warpath, she captured Prince Phillip, but her inflated ego proved to be her downfall; as she gloated over her triumph, Phillip escaped and ultimately went on to defeat her. Maleficent is obviously possessed of strong magical powers, but somehow couldn't find Aurora in hiding for sixteen years, leaving the search to her trusted raven, Diablo.

## CAREER

**FILMOGRAPHY:**
*Sleeping Beauty,* 1959
*Mickey's House of Villains,* 2002

**HONORS AND AWARDS:**
Named "Number One Villain" by
UltimateDisney.com in *The Top
Disney Villain Countdown*

# CRUELLA DE VIL

## THE FACTS

**NAME:** Cruella De Vil

**VOICED BY:**
Betty Lou Gerson (1961);
Susan Blakeslee (2003)

**LIVE-ACTION MODEL:**
Mary Wickes

**PARTNERS IN CRIME:** Horace and Jasper Badun

**DESCRIPTION:** Wealthy, sophisticated, erratic, ruthless

**DOES NOT WORK WELL WITH:**
Anyone or anything, really

**SUMMARIZING PHRASE:**
"Miserable, darling, as usual. Perfectly wretched."

**METHOD OF MENACE:**
Misguided pursuit of fashion

**SELFISH, SPOILED, AND LACKING SELF-CONTROL, CRUELLA DISPLAYS** an abrasive personality, a terrible temper, outlandish taste, and cruelty without concern or remorse. Fur coats are Cruella's only love in life. She adores fur, "absolutely lives for it," and the fur she lives for most of all is of the spotted variety—Dalmatian, that is. Roger and Anita's Dalmatians, to be precise. "Such perfectly beautiful coats," she's known to purr as she plots, thinking how much better those spots would look on her. She cares not that Pongo and Perdita's tiny pups are rather *attached* to that fur—nor that they are *not* for sale, at any price. She is resigned to doing whatever it takes to get those coveted coats. For while Cruella lives for fur, any pups that wear it…well, she doesn't give them much thought.

*REMEMBER! Cruella is impervious to outside ideas! (It's "never her fault.")*

C 89

Although her character originated in the Dodie Smith novel _The Hundred and One Dalmatians_, Cruella De Vil was further developed by Marc Davis.

**FILMOGRAPHY:**
One Hundred and
  One Dalmatians, 1961
101 Dalmatians, 1997
  (TV series)
Mickey's House of Villains, 2002
101 Dalmatians II: Patch's
  London Adventure, 2003

7

**A NOTE FROM**
# FRANK AND OLLIE,
VILLAINS DEPT.

...diabolical but not
a schemer, she never
thought anything over,
reacting instead in
purely emotional ways.

# HORACE AND JASPER BADUN

**VOICED BY:** Frederick Worlock (Horace), J. Pat O'Malley (Jasper)

**ON THEIR OWN, THE BADUNS—MEAN, ARGUMENTATIVE, SMALL-** time crooks—would no doubt have limited their activities to petty crimes and simple burglaries and thefts. But as crooks-for-hire under Cruella, Horace and Jasper are goaded into elaborate criminal activities that are, quite honestly, beyond their abilities and intelligence.

# EXTRA-EVIL VILLAINS ▶ URSULA

## THE FACTS

**NAME:** Ursula

**ALSO KNOWN AS:** The Sea Witch

**ALIAS:** Vanessa

**VOICED BY:** Pat Carroll

**RELATIVES:** Morgana (sister)

**HENCH-EELS:** Flotsam and Jetsam

**DESCRIPTION:** Flair, flamboyance, and theatricality—with a touch of con-artistry

**WORKS WELL WITH:** Eels, imprisoned souls

**DOES NOT WORK WELL WITH:** Prince Eric, King Triton

**METHOD OF MENACE:** Artfully channeled madness and a lair full of tricks

## DESCRIPTION

**BEJEWELLED AND POUTING LIKE AN OVERWEIGHT, OVER-RICH, OVER-** pampered, over-the-top society hostess gone mad, Ursula seems capable of expressing only one genuine emotion: wrath. Her every movement is a deceitful artifice, as if she's constantly performing for an audience. Her vile hobby of collecting souls in her morbid garden so that they can suffer constant humiliation is utterly in keeping with her society-hostess-from-hell persona.

When anger does bring out her true personality, the effects are staggering. And when she finally changes into a giant, towering up through the waves and over puny mortals, the extent of her fury is quite breathtaking.

*as Vanessa* ↗

"Life's full of tough choices, isn't it?"

↑ Morgana, her sister

**FILMOGRAPHY:**
The Little Mermaid, 1989
The Little Mermaid, 1992–1994
   (TV series)

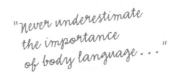

"Never underestimate the importance of body language . . ."

An octopus from Disney's nature film <u>Monsters of the Deep</u> served as a live-action model for Ursula and her swirling tentacles. (The inspiration for her buxom upper half remains unknown.)

# JAFAR

## THE FACTS

**NAME:** Jafar

**VOICED BY:** Jonathan Freeman

**PARTNER IN CRIME:** Iago
(a loudmouthed parrot)

**DESCRIPTION:** Sly, cunning,
and deceitful, with broad
shoulders, an elastic mouth,
haughty eyebrows, and an
expressive hieroglyph of
a beard

**FIENDISH DESIRES:** A short
list, really: limitless treasure,
universal magical powers, and
the hand of Princess Jasmine
in marriage

*Artist Andreas Deja based Jafar's looks on Marc Davis's design for Maleficent (of Sleeping Beauty fame).*

**TO SAY THAT THE SCHEMING JAFAR IS A NASTY PIECE OF WORK WOULD**
be understating the truth. That he is evil, there is no doubt; in fact, he is
the worst sort of traitor, betraying the Sultan while pretending to be a
faithful adviser.

In a cruel mirroring of the Genie's shape-shifting performance, Jafar
went through quite a terrifying diversity of threatening forms as Aladdin
waged battle with him to save the Sultan and Jasmine from Jafar's enchantment. Jafar's greatest moment of cruelty came when Jasmine was seeking
out her true love; with utmost callousness, Jafar lied and told her that Aladdin
had already been executed. Ultimately his lust for power led to his defeat,
and he was forced into less-than-spacious accommodations.

## CAREER

**FILMOGRAPHY:**
*Aladdin*, 1992
*Aladdin: The Return
   of Jafar*, 1994
*Aladdin*, 1994
   (TV series)
*Mickey's House of Villains*, 2002

## A NOTE FROM
# FRANK AND OLLIE,
### VILLAINS DEPT.

Jafar was using everything from his guards to the most potent magic to gain complete control of anyone who stood in the way of his plans.... Jafar could have been played more seriously, but the picture would not have been as bright and spirited. He was a storybook villain who did not have to prove how mean and odious he was.

# IAGO

**VOICED BY:** Gilbert Gottfried

**GENERALLY OBSEQUIOUS, THE BRASSY** little bird seldom has difficulty voicing his opinions or criticizing his master's failings. Iago's loyalty to Jafar is fragile at best.

# SCAR

## THE FACTS

**NAME:** Scar

**VOICED BY:** Jeremy Irons

**SIBLINGS:** Mufasa (brother)

**OTHER CLOSE RELATIVES:** Simba (nephew)

**PARTNERS-IN-CRIME:** Shenzi, Banzai, and Ed (hyenas)

**DESCRIPTION:** Deceptive, witty, sly, dastardly

**WORKS WELL WITH:** Hyenas

**DOES NOT WORK WELL WITH:** Anyone else

**SPECIAL SKILL:** Always prepared

**FIENDISH DESIRE:** To usurp his brother's throne and rule the Pride Lands

**CO-STAR COMMENT:** "He'd make a very handsome throw rug." (Zazu)

**SCAR, BROTHER OF THE KING AND UNCLE TO THE PRINCE, LACKS POWER** but suffers no shortage of pride. Consumed by a desire to be important, Scar's bitterness runs rampant in his ambition to claim Pride Rock's throne. Scar is slimy, seductive, and willing to do *anything* to rule—even if it means employing the evil hyenas and killing his brother, Mufasa, and his nephew, Simba.

Shamelessly, Scar dared young Simba to visit the forbidden Elephant Graveyard, where three hungry hyenas—Shenzi, Banzai, and Ed—awaited Simba and his friend, Nala. Fortunately, just as the hyenas were about to attack, Mufasa roared to the rescue and saved the cubs. But Scar didn't stop there. He initiated a wildebeest stampede that killed Mufasa, and then blamed Simba for his father's death. "Run far away, Simba, and never come back!" he warned the frightened cub. Chased by the hyenas, Simba disappeared into the endless savannah, leaving Scar as king of the Pride Lands! As bad guys will do, Scar let "his" kingdom slip into desperate trouble and allowed the goose-stepping hyenas to run wild. Food supplies were soon depleted and starvation and ruin spread across the land. (As kings go, he's abysmal.)

*Zazu* ↗

*Unlike the other lions in the film, Scar's claws are always displayed.*

## CAREER

**FILMOGRAPHY:**
The Lion King, 1994

The hyenas' marching was inspired by Leni Riefenstahl's 1935 *Triumph des Willens*.

EXTRA-EVIL
VILLAINS ▶ # HADES

*Hades has long been a fearsome figure to those still living; in no hurry to meet him, many are reticent to swear oaths in his name. (To many, simply saying the word "Hades" is frightening.)*

## THE FACTS

**NAME:** Hades

**VOICED BY:** James Woods

**(PART-TIME) SIGNIFICANT OTHER:** Persephone (daughter of Demeter and Zeus)

**FATHER:** Cronus (a Titan)

**MOTHER:** Rhea (also a Titan)

**SIBLINGS:** Hestia, Demeter, and Hera (sisters); Poseidon and Zeus (brothers)

**HENCH-THINGS:** Pain and Panic

**DESCRIPTION:** Ruthless, violent, rapacious, hot-headed

**FIENDISH DESIRE:** To rule the cosmos

**SPECIAL NOTE:** This is one god you don't want to get steamed up....

## A NOTE FROM
## JAMES READER,
### DIRECTOR

His scheming is almost Faustian, making deals with mortals (and indeed, half-mortals) with their souls as the prize...Of course, his schemes are all bound to fail, because like all true villains he undervalues the true power of love.

**BECAUSE OF HIS DARK AND MORBID PERSONALITY, HADES IS NOT ESPECIALLY** liked by either the gods or the mortals. He is described as "fierce and inexorable," and of all the gods he is by far most hated by mortals.

This irascible Lord of the Underworld wants nothing more than to replace Zeus on his Olympic throne, but pesky Hercules is always getting in the way. Hades can be a smooth character and is quick with a wisecrack, but he blows his top if he doesn't get his way, and then—watch out!

**FILMOGRAPHY:**
Hercules, 1997
Hercules, 1998
   (TV series)
Hercules: Zero To Hero, 1999
Mickey's House of Villains, 2002

Hades' weapon was a two-pronged fork, which he used to shatter anything that was in his way or not to his liking (much as Poseidon did with his trident). This ensign of his power was a staff with which he drove the shades of the dead into the lower world.

# PAIN AND PANIC

**VOICED BY:** Bobcat Goldthwait (Pain), Matt Frewer (Panic)

**AS IS OFTEN THE CASE WITH A VILLAIN'S** henchmen, hapless Pain and Panic aren't exactly all together in the intelligence department. Their idiotic mistakes and mishaps frequently bring the brunt of Hades' wrath.

When the ancient Greeks prayed to Hades, they banged their hands on the ground to be sure he would hear them.

← pain

panic →

**EXTRA-EVIL VILLAINS: Hades**

MYTHICAL OR LEGENDARY ▶ # RAFIKI

*The Swahili translation for "Rafiki" is "friend."*

## THE FACTS

**NAME:** Rafiki

**VOICED BY:** Robert Guillaume

**DESCRIPTION:** Crooked and bent with age, wise, knowledgeable, dignified but eccentric—often seemingly silly...or a bit mad

**WORKS WELL WITH:** All the animals of the Pride Lands

**FAVORITE PHRASE:** "Asante sana, squash banana. Wewe nugu, mimi apana." ("Thank you very much, squash banana. You're a baboon and I'm not.")

*Story person Brenda Chapman wrote down the "Asante sana..." jingle after hearing it from a guide during a trip to Africa.*

**RAFIKI IS A WISE OLD MANDRILL AND THE TRIBAL MEDICINE MAN, OR** shaman, of the Pride Lands. He travels his own road, sings his own songs, and knows what he knows. After anointing the royalty of the newborn lion cub Simba, Rafiki wandered off on his mystical way...only to return in time to guide Simba back to the path of his legacy and destiny.

*Tsidii Le Loka played Rafiki in the Original Broadway Cast of "The Lion King"— in which Rafiki is a female.*

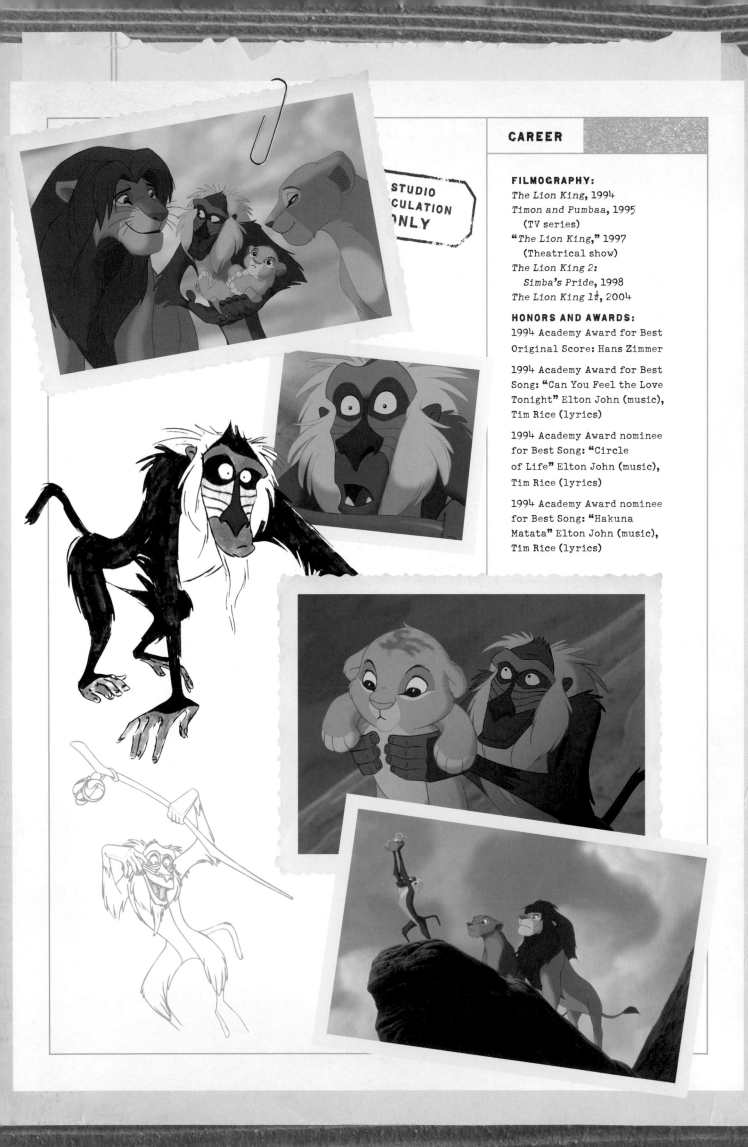

## CAREER

**FILMOGRAPHY:**
*The Lion King,* 1994
*Timon and Pumbaa,* 1995
   (TV series)
"*The Lion King,*" 1997
   (Theatrical show)
*The Lion King 2:*
   *Simba's Pride,* 1998
*The Lion King 1½,* 2004

**HONORS AND AWARDS:**
1994 Academy Award for Best
Original Score: Hans Zimmer

1994 Academy Award for Best
Song: "Can You Feel the Love
Tonight" Elton John (music),
Tim Rice (lyrics)

1994 Academy Award nominee
for Best Song: "Circle
of Life" Elton John (music),
Tim Rice (lyrics)

1994 Academy Award nominee
for Best Song: "Hakuna
Matata" Elton John (music),
Tim Rice (lyrics)

# HERCULES, MEG, PHILOCTETES

## THE FACTS

**NAME:** Hercules

**VOICED BY:** Tate Donovan (speaking), Roger Bart (singing)

**BIRTHPLACE:** Ancient Greece

**SIGNIFICANT OTHER:** Megara

**FATHER:** Zeus

**MOTHER:** Hera

**FOSTER PARENTS:** Amphitryon and Alcmene

**HORSE:** Pegasus

**DESCRIPTION:** Strong, brave, young

## CAREER

**FILMOGRAPHY:**
Hercules, 1997
Hercules, 1998
  (TV series)
Hercules: Zero To Hero, 1999

## HERCULES

OFFICIAL DOCUMENTS

**AS THE SON OF THE KING OF THE GODS AND THE STRONGEST BEING** in the world, Hercules should have it made. But a bungled kidnapping by Hades' henchmen left him stranded on Earth as the adopted son of human parents, and Hercules grew up with no idea of his divine origins—only the feeling that he didn't fit in.

After the gawky teen finally learned his father's identity, he was forced to battle a series of monsters sent by Hades. With the help of his reluctant "hero trainer," Philoctetes, and the magical winged horse Pegasus, Hercules became a superstar and a media darling—but what made him a real hero was his self-sacrifice for Megara, the woman he loves.

## THE FACTS

**NAME:** Megara

**ALSO KNOWN AS:** Meg

**VOICED BY:** Susan Egan

**SIGNIFICANT OTHER:** Hercules

**FATHER:** Creon, King of Thebes

**DESCRIPTION:** Tough, witty, resourceful

## CAREER

**FILMOGRAPHY:**
*Hercules*, 1997
*Hercules*, 1998
   (TV series)
*Hercules: Zero To Hero*, 1999

# MEG

**A HEROINE WITH AN ATTITUDE, MEGARA IS ALWAYS QUICK WITH A WISECRACK.** Although she began her career as an assistant to Hades, she quickly fell for the hunky Hercules and refused to sell him out to her evil boss. To save her new love, Megara had to undo the deception she started.

## THE FACTS

**NAME:** Philoctetes

**ALSO KNOWN AS:** Phil

**VOICED BY:** Danny DeVito

**DESCRIPTION:** No-nonsense, wisecracking; an acerbic realist

**TRAINER TO:** Odysseus, Perseus, Theseus, other "yeuseus"

## CAREER

**FILMOGRAPHY:**
*Hercules*, 1997
*Hercules*, 1998
   (TV series)
*Hercules: Zero To Hero*, 1999

# PHILOCTETES

**PHILOCTETES, A SMART-ALECK** satyr, is Zeus's go-to "hero trainer." (Although you'd never guess it from his somewhat petite and squatty physical dimensions, grotesque physiognomy, and negative overall attitude!)

# RELUCTANT DRAGON

## THE FACTS

**NAME:** Reluctant Dragon

**VOICED BY:** Barnett Parker

**BOY:** Boy

**DESCRIPTION:** The kind with wings, teeth, tails, claws, scales—all those dragon-like details

## CAREER

**FILMOGRAPHY:**
The Reluctant Dragon, 1941

*The Reluctant Dragon is based on Kenneth Grahame's short story of the same name, first published in Dream Days (1898).*

THE
BIG FEATURE SHOW
WITH A THOUSAND SURPRISES!

Walt Disney's
THE
RELUCTANT
DRAGON
Robert BENCHLEY

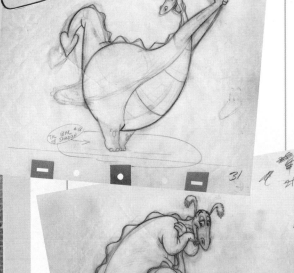

**HUGE AND PEAR-SHAPED, TALL AND GREEN, WITH EXCELLENT DICTION** and perfect manners, the Reluctant Dragon is predisposed toward personal hygiene and attendant modesty, poetry, vocalizing, flute-playing, picnics, and other pastimes of gentle refinement. He won't fight, and never has. Hasn't an enemy in the world (too lazy to make them).

*It's been said that portions of The Reluctant Dragon were redone to address objections from the Motion Picture production Code. The dragon's navel purportedly had to be removed before the film could pass.*

# ELLIOTT

## THE FACTS

**NAME:** Elliott

**ALSO KNOWN AS:** Pete's Dragon

**VOICED BY:** Charlie Callas

**BOY:** Pete

**DESCRIPTION:** Fun-loving, friendly, devoted—but fire-breathing

## CAREER

**FILMOGRAPHY:**
*Pete's Dragon*, 1977

Originally, Elliott was to remain invisible throughout most of the film. However, members of the studio animation department lobbied Studio bosses to increase his visibility. At first, he was going to be revealed only at the end, but ultimately his screen time was increased to twenty-two minutes.

**ELLIOTT HAS THE HEAD OF A CAMEL, THE NECK OF A CROCODILE,** and the ears of a cow. Big, tall, and green (with pink wings and hair), he is often invisible to everyone except his friend Pete. He's loyal and loving, but capable of being fierce and protective, and sensitive. He also projects a sense of humor and a love of fun. Elliott is also capable of extraordinary grace for his size (and even flight), despite his common clumsiness.

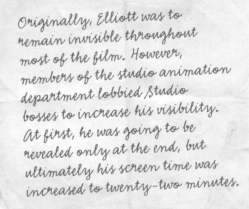

# TALL-TALE TALENT

## THE FACTS

**NAME:** Johnny Appleseed

**ALSO KNOWN AS:** John Chapman

**VOICED BY:** Dennis Day

**DESCRIPTION:** Humble, pious, enthusiastic, and hopeful

## CAREER

**FILMOGRAPHY:**
*Melody Time*, 1948

## JOHNNY APPLESEED

"Johnny Appleseed" was a genuine historic figure (1774–1845) who traveled the Ohio River Valley for forty years, planting orchards and preaching the gospel.

**AS A PUNY, PIGTAILED, SIMPLE FARMER WEARING A VEST AND APRON** and looking after his orchards, Johnny realized he didn't have the hardy constitution of the westward-bound pioneers, but he wanted to contribute to the growth of the nation anyhow. So he made it his mission to wander the great unknown, planting apple seeds as he went.

## THE FACTS

**NAME:** Pecos Bill

**TALE TOLD BY:** Roy Rogers and the Sons of the Pioneers

**SIGNIFICANT OTHER:** Slue Foot Sue

**HORSE:** Widowmaker

**FATHER:** A coyote

**MOTHER:** A she-coyote

**SIBLINGS:** Lots of little coyotes

**DESCRIPTION:** Big of chin and frame, apparently a little smaller in brain

## CAREER

**FILMOGRAPHY:**
*Melody Time*, 1948

## PECOS BILL

**A ROOTIN' TOOTIN' COWBOY IN THE CLASSIC** vein, Pecos Bill was raised by animals in the Western wilds, outloped the antelope, outjumped the jackrabbit, and generally won the West single-handedly—lassoing a rain cloud to make the Gulf of Mexico, digging out the Rio Grande, and riding a cyclone into legend.

## THE FACTS

**NAME:** Paul Bunyan

**VOICED BY:** Thurl Ravenscroft

**OX:** Babe

**CLOSE FRIENDS:** Cal McNab, Chris Crosshaul, Shot Gunderson

**DESCRIPTION:** Tall (sixty-three axe-handles high), dark, and dressed for serious lumberjacking work

## CAREER

**FILMOGRAPHY:**
"Paul Bunyan," 1958

# PAUL BUNYAN

French Canadians began telling tales of Paul Bunyan in the 1830s. "Bonyenne" is a French-Canadian expression of surprise and astonishment meaning "good grief" or "my goodness."

**WHEN A FEARSOME STORM WASHED A VAST WOODEN CRADLE ASHORE,** inside was an equally vast baby boy. He was named "Paul Bunyan" and cared for by the townspeople. He grew to become a giant of a man, the hero of the towns, and a mighty legend of the Northwest.

## THE FACTS

**NAME:** John Henry

**VOICED BY:** Geoffrey Jones

**SIGNIFICANT OTHER:** Polly (wife)

**DESCRIPTION:** A mighty man with a strong steel hammer (forged from the chains of his slavery), a powerful will, and an indomitable spirit

## CAREER

**FILMOGRAPHY:**
"John Henry," 2000

# JOHN HENRY

The legend of John Henry originated around 1870 among the miners drilling the Big Bend Tunnel of the Chesapeake & Ohio Railway in West Virginia. While he may or may not be a real character, Henry became an important symbol of the working man.

**JOHN HENRY, A FREED SLAVE, HAPPENED ACROSS** a railroad project where a crew of other freed slaves had been promised land if they could finish by a deadline. The crew members were exhausted and unable to continue, but Mighty John, with the strength of ten men, revitalized them all.

Despair returned when the railroad sent a steam hammer to replace the crew. So John proposed a challenge: man against machine. After a heroic effort—including boring a tunnel through solid rock—John won...but, sadly, he then died in his wife's arms.

# ROLE CALL OF ANIMATED CHARACTERS

**STANDARDS:**
Mickey Mouse
Minnie Mouse
Goofy
Donald Duck
Daisy Duck
Pluto
Horace Horsecollar
Clarabelle Cow
Clara Cluck
Morty
Ferdie
Max
Huey
Dewey
Louie
Scrooge McDuck
Ludwig Von Drake
Chip
Dale
Pete

**SNOW WHITE (1937):**
Snow White
Queen/Hag
The Prince
Huntsman
The Spirit of
    the Magic Mirror
Doc
Grumpy
Sleepy
Sneezy
Happy
Bashful
Dopey

**PINOCCHIO (1940):**
Pinocchio
Geppetto
Jiminy Cricket
The Blue Fairy
Cleo
Figaro
J. Worthington
    Foulfellow
Gideon
Stromboli
Coachman
Monstro the Whale

**DUMBO (1941):**
Dumbo
Timothy Q. Mouse
Ringmaster
Casey Jr.
Mrs. Jumbo

**THE RELUCTANT
DRAGON (1941):**
The Reluctant Dragon
Baby Weems
Donald Duck
Slim
Goofy

**BAMBI (1942):**
Bambi
Bambi's mother
Thumper
Flower
Miss Skunk
Friend Owl
Faline
Aunt Ena
The Great Prince
    of the Forest
Ronno

**SALUDOS
AMIGOS (1943):**
Goofy
Donald Duck
José Carioca

**THE THREE
CABALLEROS (1945):**
Donald Duck
Panchito
José Carioca

**SONG OF THE
SOUTH (1946):**
Brer Fox
Brer Rabbit
Brer Bear

**MELODY TIME (1948):**
Johnny Appleseed
Pecos Bill
Slue Foot Sue
Widowmaker
Little Toot
Donald
José Carioca

**THE ADVENTURES
OF ICHABOD AND
MR. TOAD (1949):**
J. Thaddeus Toad
Mole
Rat
Badger
Ichabod Crane
Katrina Van
    Tassel
Brom Bones

**CINDERELLA (1950):**
Cinderella
Prince Charming
Lady Tremaine,
    the Stepmother
Anastasia
Drizella
Fairy Godmother
King
Grand Duke

Lucifer
Bruno
Gus
Jaq
Mert
Bert
Suzy
Perla
Luke

**ALICE IN
WONDERLAND (1951):**
Alice
Alice's sister
Dinah
    (Alice's kitten)
White Rabbit
Mad Hatter
March Hare
Dormouse
Walrus
Carpenter
Queen of Hearts
King of Hearts
Tweedledum
Tweedledee
Cheshire Cat
Caterpillar

**PETER PAN (1953):**
Peter Pan
Captain Hook
Mr. Smee
Crocodile
Tinker Bell
The Lost Boys:
    Slightly
    Rabbit
    The Raccoon Twins
    Cubby
    Tootles
Tiger Lily
Wendy Darling
John Darling
Michael Darling
Nana

### LADY AND THE TRAMP (1955):

Lady
Tramp
Jock
Trusty
Jim Dear
Darling
Aunt Sarah
Si
Am
Tony
Joe
Dogs in the Pound:
  Boris (Russian
    wolfhound)
  Peg (Pekingese)
  Pedro (Chihuahua)
  Bull (English
    bulldog)
  Dachsie (dachshund)
Lady and Tramp's
puppies:
  Scamp
  Scooter
  Fluffy
  Ruffy

### SLEEPING BEAUTY (1959):

Princess Aurora
  (Briar Rose)
King Stefan
Queen
Fauna
Flora
Merryweather
King Hubert
Prince Phillip
Samson (Phillip's
  horse)
Maleficent
Diablo (raven)

### 101 DALMATIANS (1961):

Pongo
Perdita
Roger Radcliffe
Anita Radcliffe
Nanny
Cruella De Vil
Pongo's and
Perdita's puppies:
  Rolly
  Patch
  Lucky
  Penny
  Pepper
  Freckles
Horace Badun
Jasper Badun
The Colonel (old
  English sheepdog)
Sergeant Tibs (cat)
Captain (horse)
Towser (bloodhound)

### SWORD IN THE STONE (1963):

Wart (Arthur)
Merlin
Madam Mim
Sir Ector
Sir Kay
Archimedes (the owl)
Sir Pelinore

### THE JUNGLE BOOK (1967):

Mowgli
King Louie
Baloo
Colonel Hathi
Kaa
Bagheera
Shere Khan
Wolves:
  Rama
  Akela
Vultures:
  Ziggy
  Buzzie
  Flaps
  Dizzy
Shanti (the girl)

### THE ARISTOCATS (1970):

Duchess
Kittens:
  Berlioz
  Toulouse
  Marie
O'Malley
Roquefort (mouse)
Frou Frou (horse)
Napoleon (dog)
Lafayette (dog)
Uncle Waldo (goose)
Abigail Gabble (goose)
Amelia Gabble (goose)
Edgar (the butler)
Scat Cat
Madame Adelaide
Bonfamille

### ROBIN HOOD (1973):

Robin Hood
Maid Marian
Prince John
King Richard
Sheriff of Nottingham
Little John
Lady Kluck
Friar Tuck
Allan-a-Dale

Trigger
Nutsey
Skippy Bunny
Tagalong
Toby Turtle
Sis
Merry Men
Sir Hiss

### THE RESCUERS (1977):

Penny
Bernard
Miss Bianca
Rufus
Madame Medusa
Snoops
Nero
Brutus
Orville
Evinrude (dragonfly)
Luke (muskrat)
Ellie Mae (muskrat)
Deacon (owl)
Deadeye (rabbit)
Digger (mole)
Gramps (turtle)

### THE FOX AND THE HOUND (1981):

Tod
Copper
Big Mama
Widow Tweed
Amos Slade
Chief
Dinky (sparrow)
Boomer (woodpecker)
Squeeks (caterpillar)
Abigail (cow)

# ROLE CALL CONTINUED

### THE BLACK CAULDRON (1985):
Taran
Eilonwy
Dallben
Hen Wen
Fflewddur Fflam
Gurgi
Witches:
  Orgoch
  Orddu
  Orwen
The Fairfolk:
  King Eidilleg
  Doli
The Horned King

### THE GREAT MOUSE DETECTIVE (1986):
Hiram Flaversham
Olivia Flaversham
Fidget
Dr. David Q. Dawson
Basil of Baker Street
Mrs. Judson
Professor Ratigan
Bartholomew
Felicia (Ratigan's cat)
Toby (basset hound)
Holmes
Watson
Queen Moustoria

### OLIVER & COMPANY (1988):
Oliver
Dodger
Louie
Tito (Chihuahua)
Einstein (Great Dane)
Francis (bulldog)
Rita (Afghan)
Fagin
Sykes
Roscoe & DeSoto
  (Dobermans)
Jenny
Winston
Georgette (poodle)

### THE LITTLE MERMAID (1989):
Ariel
King Triton
Sebastian
Ariel's sisters:
  Aquata
  Andrina
  Arista
  Attina
  Adella
  Alana
Flounder
Scuttle
Prince Eric
Max (Eric's sheepdog)
Grimsby
Ursula/Vanessa
Flotsam & Jetsam
Chef Louis

### THE RESCUERS DOWN UNDER (1990):
Cody
Bernard
Miss Bianca
Nelson (echidna)
Faloo (grey kangaroo)
Marahute (golden
  eagle)
Joanna (monitor
  lizard)
Percival McLeach
Chairmouse
Wilbur
Jake Sparky (fly)

Twister (snake)
Frank (frilled lizard)
Krebbs (koala)
Red (red kangaroo)
Polly (platypus)

### BEAUTY AND THE BEAST (1991):
Belle
Beast/Prince
Gaston
LeFou
Maurice
Phillipe (horse)
Lumiere
Cogsworth
Mrs. Potts
Chip
Featherduster
Wardrobe
Footstool
Monsieur D'Arque

### ALADDIN (1992):
Aladdin
Abu
Princess Jasmine
Sultan
Rajah
Jafar
Iago
Genie
Magic Carpet

### THE LION KING (1994):
Simba
Mufasa
Sarabi
Nala
Serafina

Rafiki
Zazu
Timon
Pumbaa
Scar
Hyenas:
  Shenzi
  Banzai
  Ed

### A GOOFY MOVIE (1995):
Goofy Goof
Maximillian Goof
  (Max)
Peter Pete
P. J. Pete
Roxanne
Stacey
Principal Mazur
Bigfoot

### POCAHONTAS (1995):
Pocahontas
Meeko (raccoon)
Flit (hummingbird)
Chief Powhatan
Kocoum
Nakoma
Grandmother Willow
John Smith
Governor John
Ratcliffe
Wiggins
Thomas
Percy (pug dog)

### THE HUNCHBACK OF NOTRE DAME (1996):
Quasimodo
Judge Claude Frollo
Gargoyles:
  Hugo
  Victor
  Laverne
Phoebus
Achilles (Phoebus's
  horse)